Francesca Alfano Miglietti (FAM)

FASHIONstatements

Interviews
with Fashion Designers

Concept and Graphic Project
Cesare Fullone

Assistant to the Project and Layout
Ignazio Bennardo

Realization
Virus Graphic, Milan

Translation
Alta Price

Copy Editor
Emanuela Di Lallo

Acknowledgments

Fausto Caletti
Ennio Capasa
Michele Ciavarella
Giancarlo Gabelli
Maurizio Marchiori
Stefano Piantini
Beppe Riboli

Luciano Cirelli, Studio Karla Otto
Franca Soncini, Galleria Photology, Milan
Nu.evo
Leti B Studio
Coppola Agency
Cristiana Gorza

The publisher is at the disposal of the entitled
parties as regards all unidentified iconographic
and literary sources.

First published in Italy in 2006 by
Skira Editore S.p.A.
Palazzo Casati Stampa
via Torino 61
20123 Milano
Italy
www.skira.net

Printed and bound in Italy. First edition

ISBN-13: 978-88-7624-687-6
ISBN-10: 88-7624-687-8

Distributed in North America by Rizzoli
International Publications, Inc., 300 Park
Avenue South, New York, NY 10010.
Distributed elsewhere in the world by Thames
and Hudson Ltd., 181A High Holborn, London
WC1V 7QX, United Kingdom.

Particular thanks are due to those who made *VIRUS* all it is: to the artists, collaborators, theorists, photographers, advertisers, readers, and to all those who, in one way or another, contributed to the spread of this virus.

contents

13 — FOREWORD

WEAR YOUR HYBRIDIZATION — 17

29 — HELMUT NEWTON

ROMEO GIGLI — 34

41 — TED POLHEMUS

STEPHAN JANSON — 45

48 — LIZA BRUCE

ANN DEMEULEMEESTER — 50

55 — ALEXANDER MCQUEEN

ANNA MOLINARI — 63

68 — MARTIN MARGIELA

DAVID LACHAPELLE — 76

81 — VICTOR BELLAISH

BARE-BREASTED — 86

96 — JEAN-PAUL GAULTIER

JESSICA OGDEN — 104

108 — VIVIENNE WESTWOOD

MATT LEHITKA **116**

119 NAOKI TAKIZAWA

COSTUME NATIONAL **124**

132 HELEN STOREY

MANUEL VASON **135**

138 DIESEL

RANKIN **146**

150 WALTER VAN BEIRENDONCK

ALAN HRANITELJ **155**

158 ARMATURE

PEPI'S **168**

172 FAUSTO PUGLISI

TRISTAN WEBBER **175**

180 KEI KAGAMI

MANUEL ALBARRAN **183**

186 CAROL CHRISTIAN POELL

JOHN WILLIE **193**

199 ALAIN MIKLI

ANTONIO BERARDI 202

208 STEP BY STEP

CYBERDOG 218

222 THIERRY MUGLER

AZZEDINE ALAÏA 229

233 DIRK BIKKEMBERGS

MONICA COPPOLA 238

244 JEREMY SCOTT

UNITED ALIENS 249

252 ETRO

FRANKIE MORELLO 259

263 COMME DES GARÇONS

ALEXSANDRO PALOMBO 270

275 ANTONIO MARRAS

CINZIA RUGGERI 280

287 BIND ME

If from your first meeting with a woman you remember her dress, it means that it was an ugly dress; if you remember the woman, it means that she had a beautiful dress.

Coco Chanel

FOREWORD

Virus is a magazine of contaminations, mutations, and relations, but
it is above all a magazine that has intertwined art, fashion, cinema,
music, video art, and theory with the tensions that bring back the
spirit of a given time—our time. They are, then, the styles and trends
of a mutated dimension, and a collection of extraordinary encounters. This book is a collection of some of the most important encounters published in the magazine, with first-hand contacts, singular
approaches, testimonials, declarations, anxieties, and the secrets of
some of the most important and significant contemporary creators of
fashion. Many of the conversations featured within have been spe-
cially translated for this occasion, as the magazine invariably presented them in their original language, so they are published in
English for the first time. Thus, *Fashion Statements* presents itself
as a collection of bodies, appointments, and abnormalities. This is a
series of proposals, passages, displacements, and escapes that stirred
up a lot of fuss and unease when they first appeared, but—as always
happens with the acceleration of time—with only a little distance
everything we presented became a virtual classic. The images and
intuitions published here have, over the last ten years, transferred
themselves by almost capillary means onto the new look now seen
everywhere in advertising, video clips, films, galleries, museums,
and the pages of trade magazines.

It was quite risky, when we began, to make art and fashion cohabitate on the pages of a single magazine; nevertheless the absence of hierarchies that *Virus* has always championed, and the tension that helped identify the elements that best determine the spirit of the age, have almost automatically marked fashion as one of the privileged places of hybridization and contamination between different idioms.

Plastic, rubber, metal, synthetic fibers, fabrics and high-tech structures (like the steel one used by Junia Watanabe that was invented by a Japanese company specialized in fibers for computer and radar technologies), fiber optics, chameleon-like changeable overalls, and leather (printed leather, tattered leather, padded leather, and leather rigid as armor), anatomies, robotics, and reinforcing garters are all exhibited here. The mutating bodies try on asymmetrical forms like a second skin—jackets that close in back like straitjackets, envelopes, helmets, and moon boots. "In the relation between man and machine it isn't very clear who is the producer and who is the product. It's not clear what mind and body are in machines that resolve themselves in codified protocol. Inasmuch as we can know ourselves in formal discourse (in biology, for example) we discover that we are cyborgs, hybrids, mosaics, chimeras," writes Donna J. Haraway in *Manifest Cyborg*. Similarly, the catwalks of the last few years present us as mutants, and it becomes immediately clear that we have already mutated.

The scene:

1982. Zora flees while chased by a Blade Runner. She wears a transparent plastic raincoat.

1995. Many people have a plastic raincoat hanging in their closet.

Is this the future? From Milan to Paris, and from Paris to New York via London, Belgium, and Holland, some of the most interesting and far-seeing stylists of the moment have transformed the catwalks into sceneries inhabited by new beings. "In the cultural space of clothing a constant battle is fought between the tendency toward stability and immobility (a tendency that is psychologically lived as justified by tradition, morality, and historic and religious considerations) and the opposite tendency toward innovation and extravagance: all this plays a role in fashion's representation," writes Juri Lotman in his precious *Culture and Explosion: Predictability and Unpredictability*. One certainty is that the fashion of the past few years has been one of the hottest thermometers of this mutation.

The tumultuous cultures of the 1990s appear in a contamination of roles and sexual identities: metamorphoses, androgyny, transvestism, transferences of identity, hermaphroditism, and transsexuality are a series of themes that intertwine and recompose all that is masculine and feminine into a grouping of phenomena that characterize and modify both the real and the imagined. In this way fashion becomes the right to change oneself. It is the passage from traditional clothing, tied to ethnicity and class, to a way of dressing that, no more divided between male and female, begins to dismantle itself and multiply into numerous variables, spanning from the most diverse materials to the attention focused on the tensions that characterize all that is contemporary. Thus fashion has given itself up as a process, diffusely distributing itself through capillary action into an explosion disseminated everywhere; it doesn't belong to a precise class in particular, nor does it promote only a few models of reference, nor is it found exclusively in the costumes of society. Clothes, objects, behaviors, and tastes have all now become a device that communicates politics, economic strategies, and the means and structures of communication itself. According to Lotman, "the insertion into fashion is a continuous process of transformation of the meaningless into the meaningful. The semiotic nature of fashion manifests itself particularly in the fact that the presence of an observer is always implied."

Fashion is a reality that belongs essentially to modernity; from the moment it appears it possesses, within the history of society, an energy capable of shattering the rigidity of tradition and unfolding itself into a continuously changing mentality.

By now it is clear that "dressing exposes a body to an ever-possible metamorphosis, and the fashion of our times has allowed itself to recount these metamorphoses . . . In this way fashion has permitted the confusion of sexual roles, made visible on the surface that which was beneath (labels, lingerie, seams), inverted the covering function of fabrics by adopting transparencies, broke the equilibriums and rigid functionalisms of traditional costume and ritual dress, and adopted intertextual citation as a constant technique—in all, in a certain sense it has rendered the body a discourse, a sign, a thing," writes Patrizia Calefato in *Mass Moda. Linguaggio e immaginario del corpo rivestito* [Mass Fashion: Idiom and the Imaginary in the Covered Body].

The body is shown here as mutated, rethought, interpreted: a changing body. Characters are seen as metaphorical mechanisms; a humanity outside of the history of definitions, no longer fixed in a single linguistic, cultural, ethnic, or sexual identity. It undergoes an incessant technological remixing of the human form, in continual discovery of its own mutating body. This body appears in the pages of books, in the scenes of films, in the projections and globs of color in works of art, in the luminous swarm of videos, on the screens of cybernetic terminals, in our redesigned objects, in the regions of desire and, looking more closely, in our own mirrors. Style, in its most serious versions, from dandies to contradictory movements, no longer offers itself as a diversion, but rather as a bona fide engagement, a form of its own vision of the world, and the surface of a reality closely joined to its substance.

The bodies that appear before us on catwalks, in magazines, in ads, but also on the street, in offices, and nightclubs, are alien bodies, designed bodies, and bodies that multiply to the nth power the body's desire. The outlines of post-atomic mutations and layerings of Japanese stylists have become icons of the contemporary, as have the sheaths of Alaïa, the extremities of McQueen, the origami forms of Mijake, the new anatomies of Comme des Garçons, and the dismantled structures of Costume National. There's more: Vivienne Westwood proposes vertiginous heights and padded behinds, Jean-Paul Gaultier produces cyborg uniforms in post-nuclear environments, Thierry Mugler brings bionic women, Margiela transforms feet into horses' hooves, and Gigli shows already-mutated metropolitan multi-ethnicities.

Certainly some of these proposals are utterly impractical, transported from the imaginaries of cinema, art, and manga into daily life, into reality.

These clothes are the outlines of a costume—the symptom of a desire to transform, and its realization through a surpassing of sex, and through the ability to transform one's own perceptive and mental universe. Every appearance is a reality, while it is the "real world," and its faith in itself, that disappears.

Francesca Alfano Miglietti (FAM)

WEAR YOUR HYBRIDIZATION

Works and Clothing for a Mutating Identity   by FAM

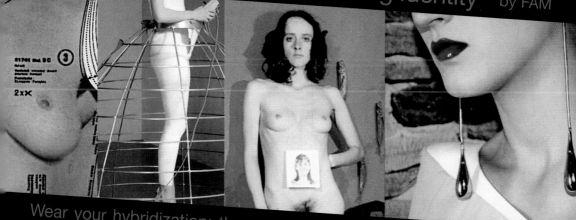

Wear your hybridization: the confines in which fashion produces designed bodies and where art places anatomies and identities into question through artworks featuring the semblances of clothes.

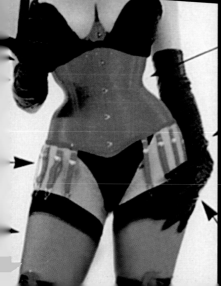
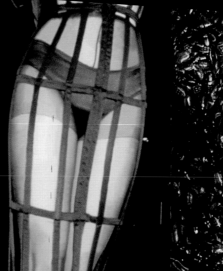

Contemporary practices of bodily modification take on the sense of a critique with regard to the global strategies of cultural anesthesia and the homogenization of body image. Permanently mutating, the body is one of many attempts at self-creation, at "re-placing" oneself in the world, generating and intervening with one's own morphology, one's own anatomy. Is there anyone who resembles his body? Anyone who corresponds to himself?

"Woman will become spec-
tral through the disarticula-
tion and deformation of her
anatomy. The *démontable*
body [able to be disassem-
bled] is the aspiration and
cold realization of female exhibitionism, which will become furiously analytical,
permitting one to show each
piece separately, and to iso-
late it in order to give it in a
meal . . ." (Salvador Dalí)

Thierry Mugler, F/W Couture 1997–1998

Stelarc, *Scanning robot / automatic arm*. Photo M. Burton

Jean-Paul Gaultier, *F/W 1995–1996*

Aliens, cyborgs, animals, organisms, and mechanisms that fuse into one another . . . anatomy is no longer a destiny, the password is no longer evolution, rather it's hybridization . . . stupor is a value . . . the penetration of experiences and knowledgeable contamination between the observer and the observed, at once subject and object of the gaze, of the cognizance, and of the conjunctions. This is a state of sensorial excitation that creates lightning-like, excessive, complex relations . . . A step, a whisper, and a caress are sensual interminglings that layer bodies atop bodies . . . Art is like a virus that propagates and infects the bodies of daily life, and life jumps across the separations between idioms and the new, mutating identities wear their own hybridizations.

Jean-Paul Gaultier, *F/W 1989–1990*

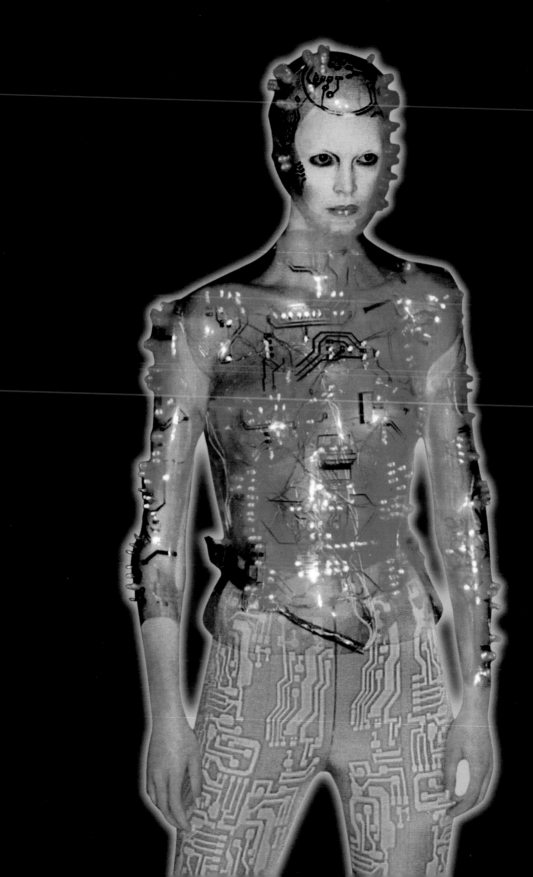

Givenchy, F/W 1999–2000

21

So art enters into the body, molding it, modifying it, exhibiting it, exposing its moods, humors, and secrets, opening it to new and more intense possibilities, creating tableaux vivants of imaginary lives that interpret histories of metropolitan folly. The point of departure is the material variety of these bodies, and the multiple forms and semblances they assume, pushed by a frenetic thirst for transformation, for the alteration of coordinates and exploration of boundaries and resources. These are realizations of a (self-)desire that fulfils itself in the radicalism of putting itself in play with its own skin and its own blood.

Mariko Mori, *Subway*, 1994

These are bodies as the subject and object of mutations—places where a hybridization that is increasingly evident, imminent, and irrevocable takes place. Fashion launches a challenge that is, above all, for the eyes, which are seduced by an imposed perception that meddles with the normalized representation of the body which has until now been portrayed as given and assumed by the media. This is a conceptual challenge that forces one to rethink the terms of the relationship between the body and its confines, between the body and its modes of producing sense, between the body and desire.

Thierry Mugler, S/S 1998. Photo Helmut Newton

23

Thierry Mugler, S/S 1998. Photo Helmut Newton

Janieta Eyre, Two Fakiris Waiting for an Audience, 1996

"A game of artificial inflation is necessary; that is to say, a systematic simulation which takes into account neither a preset state of the world nor a physics or anatomy of bodies." (Jean Baudrillard)

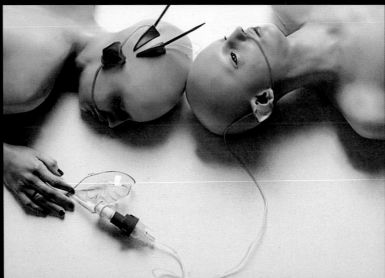

Reuven Cohen, Babylon: Norbert 1, 2, 1996

Jana Sterbak, *Remote Control II*, 1989

"Why not walk on your head, with your breasts, see through your skin, breath with your belly: the simple Thing, the Entity, the Full Body, the stationary Voyage, Anorexia, cutaneous Vision, Yoga, Krishna, Love, Experimentation . . . To find the Body without Organs (BwO) is a question of life or death, of youth and old age, of sadness and happiness. It is here that everything is on the line." (Gilles Deleuze and Félix Guattari)

Marcel.lí Antúnez Roca, *Epiphania*, 1999

Thierry Mugler, *Robot Couture, Cirque d'Hiver*, March 1995

Jean-Paul Gaultier, S/S 1989

Art as a brand of hybridization that is concentrated on becoming rather than on being, which sets itself to observing the object through the evidence of a process coming to its culmination. Transformed bodies that live in the altered systems of this era that has stopped following the nightmares of the preservation of the species. Hybridization is the instrument of the body's process of becoming, and of its mutation into something else—hybrid bodies resulting from the combination of different elements.

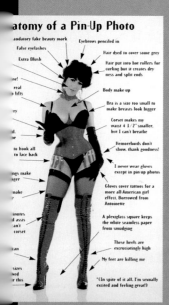

Anatomy of a Pin-Up Photo

Mandatory fake beauty mark
False eyelashes
Extra Blush

...ne!
real
...s lifts
...ry

...d.
...ne
to hook all
to lace back

...ngs make
...ager
...make

...inutes
...d assis
...an't
corset

...an

...sizes
...ved
...r this

Eyebrows penciled in
Hair dyed to cover some grey
Hair put into hot rollers for
curling but it creates dryness and split ends

Body make up

Bra is a size too small to make breasts look bigger

Corset makes my waist 4 1/2" smaller, but I can't breathe

Hemorrhoids don't show, thank goodness!

I never wear gloves except in pin up photos

Gloves cover tattoos for a more all American girl effect. Borrowed from Antoinette

A plexiglass square keeps the white seamless paper from smudging

These heels are excruciatingly high

My feet are killing me

"(In spite of it all, I'm sexually excited and feeling great!)"

Annie Sprinkle, *Anatomy of a Pin-up Photo*, 1997
Photo Zorro, design K. Gates

Jean-Paul Gaultier, S/S 1990

HELMUT NEWTON

Exasperatingly high stiletto heels, sadomaso-chistic equipment and statuary beauties: an en-counter with Helmut Newton, the creator of photo-graphs on the border between dream and nightmare.

Self-portrait with wife and models, Paris, 1981. Courtesy of Galleria Photology, Milan

Teresa Macrì: With you, who have been called the Photographer of Beauty, I'd like to focus on the concept of ugliness. In an essay dated 1853 Karl Rosenkranz, who was a philosopher one could call anything but radical, claimed that ugliness is a part of beauty, or beauty's "negative double." What do you think about that?

Helmut Newton: Unfortunately I don't know that essay. As for the label I've been given, it's simplistic and partial. If we're having a discussion of categories, ugliness fascinates me, in reality, as much as beauty, and it interests me in all its manifestations: from art, to music, to philosophy. Actually, ugliness interests me above all in its most extreme phase.

Could you give me an example of ugliness?

I don't know, at the moment only examples of contemporary architecture come to mind, where it seems to me that this quality is abundantly expressed, but I don't wish to name names.

Well, alright, talk to me about beauty . . .

Jean Moreau was very beautiful, for example. If you look, then, at my photographic book *Big Nudes*, there is a photograph of a woman I've known for many years, Violeta Sanchez, that men find repugnant because she doesn't follow the classic stereotype: she has a nose out of a Velázquez painting, very small breasts, and beautiful legs. For me, Violeta represents beauty.

But more commonly you choose canonically beautiful women, then you esthetically direct them, or rather construct them.

I detest the word esthetic, but it's true that I do a work of construction.

So, given that you're a constructor of photographic scenes, how is it that you met Andy Warhol (in the famous 1974 photograph), who is the ideologue of artifice par excellence—the inventor of himself?

Warhol was genial. Our meeting was, in any case, natural, in the sense that I photographed him while he slept. Andy had just arrived in New York and was exhausted. In the photo you're referring to he seems almost dead.

Another strong component of your seductive visual repertory is the use of fetish. But don't you believe that women are liberating themselves from these superstructures and that it's rather a question of a masculine subcultural inheritance?

Yes, I do believe that; but see, you yourself said I am a constructor, and fetishes are technically useful to me. Stiletto heels, for example, serve to bring out the leg muscles. The body hasn't any tension if it's in its natural state. And then some fetishes fascinate me.

The sets you construct at times aim for a certain vulgarity. What is your relationship to vulgarity; is it just a formal given, a constructive excess, or what?

I adore vulgarity: it represents the opposite of banality, which I absolutely disdain. Excess becomes kitsch, which has nothing to do with bad taste.

Yes, but your kitsch, all told, is very mental, it is your way of distancing from approval. It's also far from Almodóvar's hints at kitsch, which are the cultural or subcultural background from which his films are born . . .

Yes, that's true; kitsch interests me as a blasphemous idea . . .

Roland Barthes defined portraitists as great mythologists: Nadar represented the French bourgeoisie at the end of the nineteenth century, Sander represented the people of pre-Nazi Germany, and Avedon portrayed high-class New Yorkers. Which classes' myth do you represent?

Definitely that of the high bourgeoisie, but only with regard to fashion photographs, not my private life.

What purpose does your photography serve?

Some people, through my photographs, will dream, and in reality that doesn't interest me; many men have told me that they masturbate looking

Jo Champa, New York, 1988. Courtesy of Galleria Photology, Milan

interview by
TERESA MACRÌ

at my photographs—I think the act of masturbation represents a strong level of emotion and active comprehension of that which the image represents. And the relationship that viewers create with my photographs is very strong; they are either loved or hated, and I'm perfectly fine with that.

Romeo Gigli was born near Faenza, Italy, in 1959. After secondary school he decided to become an architect. He traveled the globe in search of new cultures and influences, and it was during these travels that he discovered his passion for fashion. In 1979, in New York, he worked as an assistant at the Dimitri Studio, where he learned tailoring and dressmaking—an invaluable experience. Since then the distinctive feature of Romeo Gigli's style has been small, discreet shoulders. Even in the 1980s, a period in search of power, when Italian fashion houses chose to use shoulder pads in jackets and coats, he remained faithful to his line. Nature is the dominant theme in his collections, which are rich with natural fibers and palettes of color that draw references and coherencies from season to season.

A person's beauty is solely interior—it's a force, an e you carry within. The beauty of a work of art is its capac own storytelling. In both cases there is no beauty if not and passions.

interview by FRANCESCA A

FAM: One of the most evident aspects of your work is a multiethnic contamination, and an ability to see the world and its inhabitants in their many facets.
Romeo Gigli: That is part of my curiosity; for me it is very important to absorb, always and invariably, the world's cultures. The cultures of the world construct your particular way of communicating, and it's a way to go beyond your own "mental home." My first trip was to India: I was eighteen years old and knew the world only through books, through "written" culture; I knew very little about the visual cultures.
What is an image?
An image is an emotion—always. It cannot be anything else, only if it's an emotion is it an image, otherwise it's just an ugly representation of something.

ROMEO
GIGLI

F/W 1994–1995. Photo Max Vadukul

Advertising campaign 1994. Photo Max Vadukul

How much does the world of contemporary images have an impact on your research?

It is difficult to succeed in representing one's own work amid a surplus of images, especially if you want to do it in a way that is different from all the rest. It is an ambitious and often impossible operation, because you are inevitably working with a structure that is already strongly organized; you work with fashion photographs, with the photographer closest to you, with

some models, etc., and all that still isn't the new project that you want to live—it's very difficult to communicate the path of images that you construct and that you discover. And how can you find an evolution in your work itself and your way of presenting it? I don't mean to say that by modifying the operations of presenting the work you've found the keystone, but perhaps you begin to find some new paths. I am looking for a way to completely absorb all that which surrounds me, and I refer to a world of information, readings, meetings, and emotions: all told, a project that absorbs you completely, in an almost hypnotic way. I'm looking for a point of view that translates, into my work, everything that for some reason attracts my attention—a multifaceted gaze that wants to communicate above all the emotion of complexity, a project that engulfs studio, emotion, design, organization, etc.

S/S 2001

What stimulates a new project for you?
I think that, independently of fashion, the job of a designer is, before all else, to harvest the latent desire in people. We should have antennae for detecting desire, and turn latent desire into a design. One of the ways to impart contemporaneity to this design is to transform it into a miniature world that contains the design itself, and all the pieces within this miniature world need to be able to live with other realities. There needs to be a total balance, and the design and its elements must be transformed in their encounters with individuals; for me single outfits are part of a story that I am telling, but they serve above all to underline the personality of their wearer, and in turn these personalities will tell and represent the story.

What are your passions?
Oh, there are so many it's quite difficult to list them; I am very passionate. For me, everything is passion: travel, research, friendship, music, cinema, and art. I am highly curious—I give myself no rest, ever.

How much do your passions have an impact on your work?
A lot: they are my emotion.

Are you able to transform your passions into designs?
Always. Everything is channeled through them, they are my filter for expressing all that, for better or worse, I think, imagine, and see.

What is beauty?
Beauty is solely interior; there cannot be a canon for beauty—beauty is strength, energy, and an interior balance, if we're talking about the beauty of a person. The beauty of a work of art, on the other hand, lies in its transmitting of its own storytelling. Whatever it is, beauty lives within a person or a work; there cannot be a manner, if there is a manner there is no beauty. The route is always the same, it passes through emotions and passions—that is the true beauty.

You have often organized artistic events, both visual and musical; how

much does the creation of others have an impact on your creation?

A whole lot; it's very important for me to pass through these curiosities, this desire to absorb and understand what is happening outside of me—this is the only way for me to design, otherwise I couldn't do it. In the same way I harvest what's happening in the world. And naturally I am interested also in creating artistic events, giving space to that which I believe in, from music to visual presentations.

Virus *is the acknowledgement that creation, imagination, and mutation can be transmitted like a contagion.*

Certainly, it's very important to think in this way. We have gone from moments of great euphoria to moments of great depression: we now need to find the instruments of a new mentality. I hope that after the Middle Ages there's still the Renaissance!

How much does art change the world?

Art is always a great gift. It is a way of discovering oneself while at the same time giving of oneself. It is always a violent operation, because you expose yourself and absolutely anything can happen to you: but you cannot do without it if you have this type of design inclination, and it's the only means of permitting the world to invent new things, new dynamics, and new energies.

There is a lot of enchantment in the stories you tell in your fashion shows: what is enchantment for you?

It is the desire to marvel, in a positive sense; it is the great desire to give something, but with great lightness. Stupor is a difficult operation, but one that fills me with joy.

Is it possible to predict our look in the twenty-first century?

Many things will happen around us, and it's impossible to predict how men and women will be in the twenty-first century. The future depends on too many things, and on the political, economic, and ecological situation. I can only hope that the twenty-first century being will be free of mental schemes. With respect to fashion I hope to no longer see people dressed in a certain way because fashion has told them that they *have to* be that way.

What is the difference between designing for a man or for a woman?

It's very different, firstly, because I am a man. Designing for a woman is always paying her homage, it's the desire to continuously give her a present; designing for a man is purely the search for a material and colors in an extremely comfortable manner. Designing for a man always brings me back to something that is already in my memory, a sort of recollection; designing for a woman is more illusory. An outfit, for me, is the need to relate oneself at the very first meeting.

How much of an impact will new technologies have in the coming years?

An extremely radical impact; this is why I say it's not possible to predict a twenty-first-century being. On a technical level everything travels at such a speed that it's unthinkable to know how tomorrow will be.

Mental ecology—how do you keep your mind clean?

By harvesting everything that surrounds me, with a door left ajar for emotions: this is a very costly operation, but it's the only one. I clean by moving around and collecting everything I encounter.

In your materials (invitations, press sheets, etc.) there is often a selection of poetic and philosophic quotes from various cultures . . .

It's a way of giving the coordinates of my story, the leg of a journey to be taken together . . .

Is there any advice you'd like to give to a magazine like Virus?

More than advice I'd like to cast a wish—that you might never lose this magnificent point of view. It's everything we need right now, a great energy that is above all a lifestyle, a way of being.

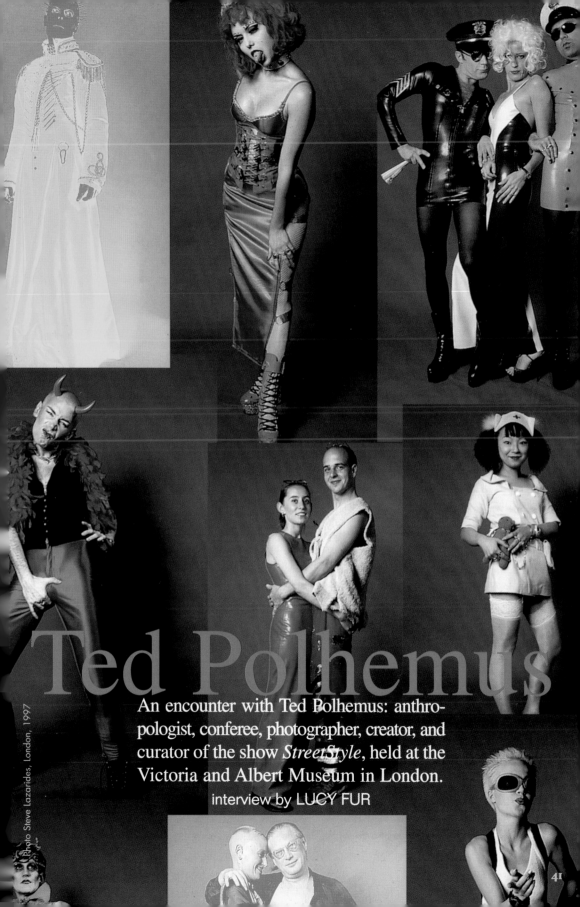

Ted Polhemus

An encounter with Ted Polhemus: anthropologist, conferee, photographer, creator, and curator of the show *StreetStyle*, held at the Victoria and Albert Museum in London.

interview by LUCY FUR

Photo Steve Lazarides, London, 1997

Lucy Fur: What is street style?
Ted Polhemus: Street style as a phenomenon has been around for over fifty years . . . but at the beginning there were very few choices: if you were black and lived in New York you could have a "Zazous," if you were white and lived in Texas you could have a western style, but there weren't any possibilities beyond these . . . Today, especially after the advent of punk at the end of the 1970s, we live in a period in which there is an incredible range of stylistic choice, there are dozens of different street styles from which one can choose, different subcultures, and different stylistic tribes. Each of these features a different way of dressing, way of living, a behavior, and a philosophy that are expressed in that way of dressing. It's as if everyone had a musical style as an accompaniment. In addition to this, the exciting aspect of our time is the variety of references we have, the great range of choice, the fact that mainstream society, through the fashion industry, is very interested in what is happening on the streets, because it must, because it's the only interesting thing, the only truly authentic and creative thing. This is what's happening now. But today it goes beyond this choice, because many people draw from what I call the "style supermarket" the entire history of street style. It's the same thing as picking a can of soup off the supermarket shelf, where you have an enormous variety in front of you: today there is a style supermarket with an extraordinary selection, and one can opt for the style he likes best and wear it for a single evening, for a month, or for the rest of his life . . . Another important thing is that new people have a bond to music . . . what I call sampling and mixing: just as in the musical realm, large sections of old music are taken, a little James Brown, a little Beethoven, a little Ravel . . . and mix. And people do the same thing in terms of style: they take necklaces associated with hippies, pair them with a rubber tank-top associated with fetishism and post-style, and add a pair of glam bell-bottomed pants from the 1970s, together with a pair of Doc Martens' boots that recall punks and skinheads. These are all the subcultures that have historically been independent from one another, and often in conflict; but today, in the extraordinary supermarket of style, all these pieces can be taken. You just open different soup cans, pour them all into a large pot, and they amalgamate, creating a new vocabulary with which you can express your ties with all the various subcultural possibilities. This is an extraordinary phenomenon that belongs to our time, speaks to us about the way in which the future can take the past and make it its own.
What is the relationship, or lack of relationship, between fashion and style? In your stylistic territory it seems that fashion has a different function from that of style; but usually media and communications connect these two terms.

Murray & Vern for the *Skin Two 3* collection, 1993.
Photo Peter Ashworth

The words *fashion* and *style* are often used as synonyms, but they are really two very different things. I believe that fashion brings with it a continual change: this year's look replaces last year's. I think that today many more people are concentrating on style, not fashion; people are looking for a small tribe, not just the youth, but also middle-aged people, rich and poor . . . Everyone is looking for a subculture to grab on to, often even a subculture within the so-called fashion industry, and within these little worlds people maintain a style—not a fashion, but a style—that goes from one year to the next. Nowadays it's no longer important what year we live in, but rather what tribe we belong to.

What is the relationship, the analogy, between a style tribe *and a normal tribe?*

That's a good question, thanks. I use the term style tribe in a very real way: punks, for example, are spread around the world, but nevertheless through their music and their way of dressing they share a sense of community and belonging. Human beings are tribal animals: this, in a certain sense, is what differentiates us from other animals and has allowed us, for better or worse, to dominate the planet, because we insert ourselves in communities that can live beyond a single generation, and therefore accumulate information. We need to think of a tribe like a computer that memorizes information: one generation learns certain things, then dies; but it's passed this information on thanks to the data memorized by the tribe. This makes human beings special, unique, and very powerful. Human nature is structured in such a way that it needs to be social, and to belong to a tribal group. Today's society isn't, in reality, a society, we don't feel that we belong to Great Britain, or America, or Italy; we're spread throughout the world, and have no sense of community, belonging, or engagement. At the same time it's worth remembering that these tribes that we've created, these style tribes of Western contemporaneity, are fundamentally very different from those in the third world, in Africa, in the Amazon, in Polynesia and so on. Only for one detail are they international: they don't have a piece of land. If you fly over the Amazon you can see, from the sky, the territory of a particular tribe; but the closer you get the more you realize that this tribe differentiates itself from others in its way of covering the body. All these people, in a true tribe, know one another, work together, and their lives depend on the lives of others. Punks, skinheads, and teddy boys are international groups of people who don't know one another, but by music, their shared way of dress, and also, ironically, because of the media—which are often justly hated because they create

Postmodern Punk
shirt: Joie & Union Jack
pants: Jimmy Jumble from
Sign of the Times, 1993.
Photo Jeremy Deller

stereotypes—so for all of these things, media included, punks, skinheads, and ravers in various parts of the world know about one another. So even if they don't know one another personally, they can feel a sense of community and belonging within an international context. The tribes of the past were limited to a particular geographic area in the world; today's style tribes have an enormous impact, because they use the media to create an international network of likeminded people.

Photo Steve Lazarides, London, 1997

Born and educated in France, after several years spent in the United States Stephan Janson arrived in Italy and opened an atelier. His fashion shows attract an ever-greater number of buyers and journalists who often confess an instinctual love of his style and his battle against the idea of a brand based on an image rather than on the reality of the clothes.

Interview by EVA PINI

STEPHAN JANSON

Eva Pini: Why do you design clothes?
Stephan Janson: Because they're indispensable.
Well, there are many other indispensable things . . .
That's true, but what happened was that when I was thirteen years old I saw a dress by Saint Laurent on the cover of *Vogue*, an haute couture dress. This episode represented a dream, a creation, the ability to create a dream, to create beauty. My mother explained what haute couture was and so I decided to be a tailor.
For who do you design? Who do you dress?
I design for myself, and do only what I want. I don't think of a type of woman particularly in harmony with my dresses; all women could be, if they were

attracted to that. There must be an emotional impulse to make you choose what to wear (or at least that's how it should be)—the same impulse that pushes me to design or to pair together single pieces the way I do. What really matters to me is the quality; my professionality demands it.

Who would you like to dress?

I never think of anyone in particular, much less of a famous person; at most I could imagine someone who wears my clothes with elegance—that is my true satisfaction. I love elegance, it's something innate: you cannot learn to be elegant even if given all the most fashionable clothing available. When I walk around Tangiers I imagine my dresses on the local women while they work; and I see them being worn with an elegance that enchants me. Only then do I seem to understand the sense of my work.

How is one of your collections born? What are the sectors of daily life from which you feel the most influenced?

Never does it come from a film. Anything that makes it to the big screen has already been conceived for the masses, and is therefore already old. A trend is not a concept, but rather a bona fide business; trends are promoted to people who believe they are stupid—but they're not, or at least they wouldn't be if they weren't kept in this void, if they were stimulated to develop their own personalities instead of homogenizing them. I come from the 1960s and I believe in the individual, I believe it's necessary to anticipate, and offer new proposals. That which inspires me most is without a doubt literature, because it leaves the imagination free to roam. Reading Elsa Morante's *La storia* [History], for example, I dreamt of dresses made of light, overlapping strata; dressing the protagonist of a book could be a stimulus to create.

I look around and see that you've surrounded yourself with a bit of Africa. What does Africa represent for you?

A faraway place, a more poetic and true dimension, where you can rediscover the simplicity of life—it takes very little to get the feeling of being happy.

But how much of an influence has African culture had on your work?

It's not so much African culture that touches me, rather the pride and vivacity of the African people that moves me, in the sense that they succeed in affecting me. I am an observer, and in Africa I can relax and allow my attention to concentrate on the colors, odors, and spaces . . . the images of Africa fill me.

What culture has influenced you the most?

None. My own. I lived first in Paris and then in New York (in the 1960s); they recognize me still in that particular way of being, in the love for rebellion. The youth had no desire to be labeled, they just wanted to live and this made everyone want to give themselves a particular identity, to differentiate themselves from others, from the plans of parents who had a preset idea of a certain type of life. The youth sought out beauty and liberty. This behavior is evident also in the fashions of the day, you understood it from the extreme simplicity of the forms; this is what I want to do, what I still feel like doing today.

What difference is there between fashion and costume?

It is a lack of personality, which is regrettably widespread, that causes people to view fashion as a mask; to give themselves an identity that uses fashion as a uniform, killing all emotional impulse to dress with inspiration and individuality; all this leads to the dominance of bad habits. Those in your generation are better; I'm always meeting more people in their twenties that I like. You're not superficial, you don't want to be labeled. So many useless values have been inflated, and one of these is certainly fashion (if I can call it a value). People give clothes a value they don't have; they've been reduced to just images without content, and the images are always stronger; but

without content they only become more dangerous and, I think, even damaging. Costume should be the expression of the changing of our time; and fashion, the expression of our time now. Unfortunately fashion has become merely business: "those who make fashion" sit down together at a table and decide which images will work this year, which will be so strong as to drag everything else along, and which will expand the business. I give myself the little luxury of not giving out images: I don't want to strike with ads, nor do I want women who seek to transmit through my clothes a look they don't possess. The longer I move on the more, for example, the photographic material of my collection drops in quality; the shows and ads should only be working tools, not a spectacle: a means, and not an end. The joke is that no one cares what Janson thinks will work this winter: after a couple of weeks they'll have already forgotten it, they remember the models, not the clothes.

Do you think this is just a phase, and that we'll return to a more realistic vision of fashion?

I don't think so. Everything today betrays a great weakness: people just want uniforms that satisfy some deep-seated need for security. That proves that today's people are of little depth: nothing is less realistic than feeling reassured by a uniform.

What is changing in the fashion system?

Industry is always better at giving us these uniforms, we're approved, and they make us think that the talent lies in successfully dictating what will work next season. On the other hand, as long as no resistance is raised the situation can't change, and the resistance lies in taking a less superficial stance. Business expands, but the concept of fashion is progressively emptying itself of all its content. I really don't care to enter this circle, and I won't hold a show anywhere that isn't my showroom. My clothes are born here, they descend into the crowd, they get looked at, and they return up here, and those who come here do so only because they're interested in what I create. It's the human dimension of my work: the product is seen for what it is, a proposal, nothing more. When I was a boy I wanted to revolutionize fashion, and today I simply want to be part of its evolution; let's just say I prefer the whispers of fashion to the screams, also because I believe that this evolution is slower that one might think (or want to make people think).

Why did you come to Italy?

For love. I feel well in Milan, now. At the beginning I was a little bothered by the general pretense that it were an international city, which it isn't; but then I let myself fall into a fascination with a type of life that can be led in a provincial city, and now I like being here.

Eva Pini: How would you describe your design style?
Liza Bruce: I seek to design without referring to the past or to any ideal. I design for a reckless woman, for a woman who doesn't want to let herself be dressed by people who consider her a doll.
Do you simply consider yourself a stylist, or do you mean to propose a new lifestyle?
The concept of lifestyle is similar to that of good taste . . . taste is subjective, and good taste quickly turns into bad taste. In the concept of lifestyle there is a sort of fascism, homogeneity, and lack of personality.
So what do you want to express with your style?
I'll respond to your question with my philosophy, my point of view that embraces every aspect of my life. Style is a matter of personality . . . and personality is an endangered species . . . so that which we now understand as style is more a question of tribal identity than anything else.
I personally think your distinct originality is visible above all in the materials you use. How do you choose them?
I look for fabrics that express optimism for the future, not nostalgia for the past . . . even if at times it could be interesting to juxtapose classic fabrics with modern ones.
What distinguishes fashion from art?
I don't think there's any difference . . . fashion can be art . . . and art is too often a fashion . . . too often it's only a question of fashion . . . and passes quickly out of fashion.
By what or whom is your work influenced?
By everything and nothing . . . and very often by the fact that I just think I don't want to be like them . . .
Do you let art in general influence you? And music?
Art in general . . . no! One or two artists . . . yes. Music in general . . . no . . . Music in general . . . yes.
What difference is there between fashion and style?
They have nothing in common. Fashion is like a sheep, style is personality.
Today the establishment is always closer to what is considered underground. Does the underground still exist?
People who think of themselves as underground are so studied and full of themselves that they might as well be actors reciting a well-contrived script. I think it was Norman Mailer who said that subversion is a tuxedo with cummerbund, and that the so-called politically correct is FASCISM.
Is fashion changing?
Nothing will change until the end of the millennium . . . There's a rampant fear that is pushing everything to take shelter in the past, in nostalgia, in the security of something predictable and boring.
What culture has had the greatest impact on you, American or European?
Cultural references don't interest me at all. In Europe everyone wants to be American and in America everyone wants to be a refined European! Thank God I feel neither European nor American. I feel like an outsider, and this is what influences me.
Do the art and fashion worlds live together in England?
The ephemeral fashion world and the ephemeral art world are sleeping with one another in England, but that's not interesting for any more than ten seconds . . . after which there's no passion, just reciprocal suspect.
What instrument do you use to make your creations known?
Me!

LIZA BRUCE

As soon as she arrived on the London scene Liza Bruce became one of the protagonists of the new Londoner style. Courtney Love and Kate Moss are among her fans. She is cultured, audacious, politically involved, and subversive. She creates provocations by designing clothes that play with female stereotypes and the preconceptions that want women "undressed." Minimal but never banal.

interview by
EVA PINI

Photo Patrick Robyn

Ann Demeulemeester

A key figure in the Belgians group, the designers who have established themselves as the most alternative innovators in the field of fashion, we speak here with Dutch designer Ann Demeulemeester, revolutionizer of form and line.

interview by EVA PINI

Eva Pini: Simple and extravagant, transgressive and elegant, and sensuous, with the back, rather than the bust, bared (brilliant!). Do opposites attract you?
Ann Demeulemeester: The opposite of a true thing is equally stimulating, and a source of inspiration. Everything a person can do lies between two extremes that are opposite one another. In making any sort of decision, one is replying to a question: where does my action belong between these two opposing extremes?
What sort of woman do you imagine wearing your clothes?
A woman who knows what she wants.
What is an image?
It is an attempt at visualizing an idea. Sometimes it works out as planned, some other times it surprises you and causes the thing to evolve.

What do you want to express with your style?
That fashion can be an interesting means for expressing one's own style.
Obviously you can do without it. I do nothing more than put forward my
own proposals!
What is modernity in current fashion?
Individuality, even if one sees regrettably little of it around.
What is changing?
The media try to make us believe that things are radically changing in fash-
ion. There are tons of people terrified of the future; and because of this one
sees a lot of retro stuff. The day that this fear disappears the real changes
will come.
Do you believe in "mutations"?
Of course, every day is different from the others.
Where do you get your inspiration?

Inspiration is a magnificent thing. It's difficult to explain where it comes from, it is smoothing given to you; if I were religious, I'd say it comes from up above.

What do you let influence you?
Both that which attracts me and that which I find repulsive. Stimuli are very important; they come primarily from people—for what they are and not, essentially, for what they do.

What is your relationship to art? Do you think all creative expressions are art? Is fashion art?
Sometimes I believe that art is the most precious thing in the world. It's absolutely faithful because it's always at your side when you most need it. In this life there are many forces that try to get you down, and art is an excellent weapon against them. Fashion and art can flirt with one another, but I'd maintain that they are two distinct things. They have one thing in common: both seek to reflect their times. Fashion has a more or less frivolous and exterior aspect; pure art is quite another matter.

What is your relationship with shoes?
Shoes have, like all accessories, a more or less fetishistic value. They're objects much more than clothes are, and their form is almost inalterable. Given that I like to work with forms, it's natural that I'd love shoes. And within a wardrobe they're important also because they greatly influence the way we move. Everyone walks with their feet, right?

Is the arrival of Belgians, Germans, and Brits in the world of fashion over the last few years important?
It proves that the world is always growing smaller.

What is beauty?
The joy of the senses.

What is the word of the future?
Love (that's eternal), hope, faith, and courage.

S/S 1990. Photo Patrick Robyn

Alexander McQueen

The new name of
the English fashion
panorama: very
young, thanks to
a design that fuses
past and present to
create an absolute-
ly contemporary
style, Alexander
McQueen is the
designer who aims
to revolutionize the
concept of fashion.

interview by
DAVIDE BRAMBILLA

Davide Brambilla: What, according to you, most influences your work?
Alexander McQueen: Nihilism and the strong aggressivity at the moment in London. Aside from art, from art history, my feelings come from the aggressivity I see on the streets.

Do you get the feeling that the art and fashion worlds are growing nearer?
On my level, yes, in a very significant way.

Do you see more as a fashion designer or as an artist?
Fashion designer.

Is there a big difference between fashion design and art?
They are two different things: one is commercial, the other is esthetic. Esthetics and business usually don't merge very well. And in any case, in the art and fashion worlds this doesn't happen; they just become ideas.

What do you think of contemporary art, and in particular of British art?
As it stands now fashion in England is finally gaining a position at the forefront. Just like Damien Hirst, the Chapman Brothers, and Mark Quinn are currently among the major protagonists of British art, some fashion designers, together with me, are becoming the protagonists of British fashion. I think above all of Hussein Chalayan and Owen Gaster: everyone who is rather inclined toward nihilism as a final goal. So aggressivity is a constant, and you have to bring forth the truth that in England the people have always been denied that. That truth that exposes one of the greatest contradictions of the moment in Great Britain: if in a political sense we've remained one of the most influential countries in the world, in reality we continue to have a management that makes us regress to the eighteenth century.

Do you think this is the principal reason for the current success of British fashion, art, and music?
British music has always been at the worldwide vanguard, without a doubt, from the Rolling Stones to Oasis.

Are there artists that could influence you with their work?
Hans Bellmer. His works are the total metaphor of the female body.

Have you ever thought of working with an artist, and, if so, who?
For the Florence Biennial they thought of pairing an artist and designer to work together, for example Julian Schnabel with Issey Miyake. I was supposed

F/W 2000–2001

to work with David Bowie, but I succeeded in getting a space all my own, and it won't be fashion. I'm creating an installation, trespassing all limits. I hope to work on it with the Chapman Brothers.

Do you like their work?
It makes you think, and that's what anything should do, everything should be thought-provoking. And if it doesn't make you think then it's not worth doing. Also in fashion, the show itself should make you reflect, it's of no use to create something that doesn't, in one way or another, inspire some emotion.

What is the relationship between your designs and the body?
It's the point of departure for everything one does as a designer: everything lies in how one proceeds. Usually I cut sections and work starting with the

S/S 2001

body as a base in such a way that, using technique, it either looks taller or shorter, smaller, fatter, or thinner.

Do you get the feeling that behavior with respect to the bodily form will be different toward the end of the millennium?

No, I don't think one can impose so much on human beings to the point of obliging them to wear clothes that don't feel good. Style will become very free, very loose, and there will always be fewer details, fewer useless meticulousness.

What do you think of transformations of the body, like in Orlan's work?

F/W 2000–2001

I understand her, and am interested in the fact that it doesn't seem to have anything to do with art, because plastic surgery has been around for years; and that there's someone who continues to underline what is good and what is bad about plastic surgery in regards to beauty or something else . . .

What is beauty to you?

It's in the eye of the beholder. It can be anything, depending on who the person is. It could be an ugly person that, for you, has something infinitely beautiful, it does not have to be a model. Beauty is precisely that which you find inside people.

It is important to live in London for you and your work?

I wouldn't want to live anywhere else; I've been almost everywhere, and I don't like New York or Paris.

You worked on Saville Row and with Romeo Gigli. Did these experiences leave their mark on you?

Saville Row, yes; Gigli did once, but doesn't anymore. I no longer want to be influenced by anyone. I try to find personal inspirations in the experiences of daily life, in what I see friends do, in what I see on the street, in art galleries, and in the past; but I don't really let myself be influenced by other fashion designers.

What relationship do you have with the fashion world?

I lived for some time in Milan. I like Milan, but I prefer London. I'm currently working a lot in Italy, because I have support there. But I prefer London, because it's there that everything happens.

Do you think your work would change if you lived elsewhere?

Perhaps it would become more aggressive, for political reasons, anyway. New York is still very racist, and then there are political problems in all countries, like Berlusconi in Italy: if he goes to government it will be a real problem for the arts. All told, just as in any other field, it's not a great world. *Mors tua, vita mea*—that's the world of fashion. For a while you're sky high, then you're down; like in any other place, sometimes it's hard and then it gets better, just like the waves of the ocean, up and down.

How do you see the future for the new generation of creative people?

It's like walking a tightrope; you could fall at any moment.

F/W 2000-2001

Anna Molinari. Photo Helmut Newton

ANNA MOLINARI

Blumarine—clothes as a biological double, a total game of signs in which seduction, eroticism, and sex appeal are played out with the irony of being taken to an extreme. Anna Molinari—the metropolitan chaos of invention, of multiple identities, and of changing singularity. This is an encounter with two of the most exuberant styles of international fashion.

conversation with
ANNA MOLINARI
and ROSSELLA TARABINI
by NORMA FAWN

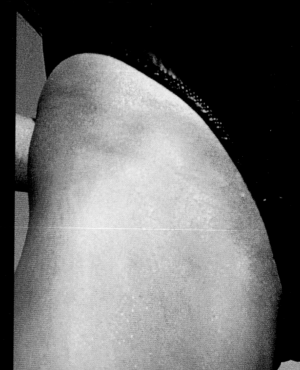

Norma Fawn: The image of femininity is sexy and ironic for Blumarine, while the women of Anna Molinari are more autonomous and seductive. Are these two worlds related?

Anna Molinari: Yes and no. Certainly they're two completely different worlds; the first bets on the option of an *abundant* femininity, chosen sexiness, sensuality as an ironic weapon, and the desire to show off, expose oneself; there is a clear reference to a certain type of cinema, and myths like Marilyn Monroe. The Anna Molinari idea of femininity is freer, less predictable, it is a matter of knowing how to change, how to fearlessly choose contradictions. But at the heart of each the real game is one of irony, not taking oneself too seriously—that's the unifying factor.

How would you define the two feminine typologies you design for?

Rossella Tarabini: One is *object* and the other is *subject*, even if the two worlds end up melding with one another in order not to remain opposites, because both are chosen identities, and because the two dimensions are interchangeable. Certainly in the *subjective typology* there is a true love of woman, while in the *objective typology* there is a true love of man . . .

Your presentations are always extremely carefully curated: artistic photographs, beautiful music . . . how much do these "other worlds" affect your creativity?

Anna Molinari: A whole lot; it's through looking and living a series of vital realities that our clothes are born. We don't think of fashion as a separate reality—actually, the common concept of fashion really bothers me, because it's a stereotype, an imposition. When I design I think of beings who have chosen to live in their own time, who experience contrasting worlds, who want to shape their own identities even through their choice of clothing.

What is custom?

Anna Molinari: Custom is the past, it's a tie to tradition. Changes in custom happen very slowly, custom changes when there are social changes, it changes after the adjustments are made, following a well-planned line of a new *norm*. Custom is a little like the *inevitable* acceptance of a change.

And fashion?

Rossella Tarabini: Fashion, even with all its banalities, is change, it's keeping your eyes open, it's being ready to change everything.

Anna Molinari: Fashion tries incredibly hard to move forward . . . it tries hard to work on an idea of transformation that is always in action.

What, to you, is perversion?

Rossella Tarabini: Normality—normality is perverse . . . Today the common ground is *strangeness*, a textbook strangeness, an "everybody's strange," a completely fake dimension made up of the stereotypes of so-called strangeness. An there's nothing worse than a reassuring strangeness!

What element of all that is contemporary most surprises you?

Rossella Tarabini: People; it's as if the majority of people were living in the past, and it seems to me that there's little wish to close with the past . . . it's as if that

Anna Molinari. Photo Helmut Newton

Photo-Helmut Newton

which was will never end . . . it's an indescribable feeling, but it's very strong, and very unsettling . . .

Anna Molinari: The thing that most surprises me is the contemporary tendency to

Blumarine. Photo Jürgen Teller

Anna Molinari. Photo Helmut Newton

Anna Molinari. Photo Helmut Newton

expect *evil*, to think that everything is the product of evil instincts; people no longer think that it's possible to expect good things from the people like them. No one is surprised by wickedness anymore, which for me, on the other hand, has always been an unexpected thing, and surprises me each time. Actually, I don't think it's possible that someone would want to do me harm. Call it naïveté, but I prefer a healthy naïveté to the disease of cynicism.

It's already possible, through the use of new technologies, to redesign one's own body. Do you ever refer to these rethought bodies when you design?

Anna Molinari: This is one of the most important transformations of our time, one of the most in-your-face symptoms of a new mental dimension . . . it's a bit true . . . when one designs clothing it's a little like redesigning the bodies!

66

Anna Molinari. Photo Helmut Newton

67

MARTIN

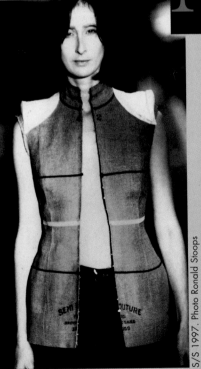

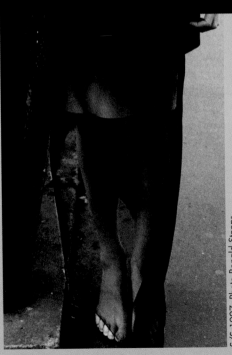

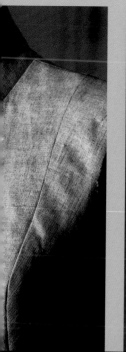

An encounter with one of the "transformers" of costume, in a dimension of contamination, infraction, rebellion, alteration, transgression, and surprise. Martin Margiela's universe is one of

MARGIELA

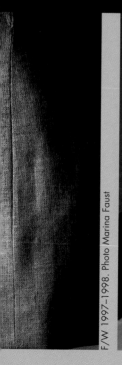

F/W 1997–1998. Photo Marina Faust

Summer 1998. Photo Barbara Katz

passions—full of images and imagination—a mutating scene in which bodies and their representations mutate, clothing and accessories become stretches, grafts, and extensions.

interview by FAM

Winter 1989–1990, Photo Ronald Stoops

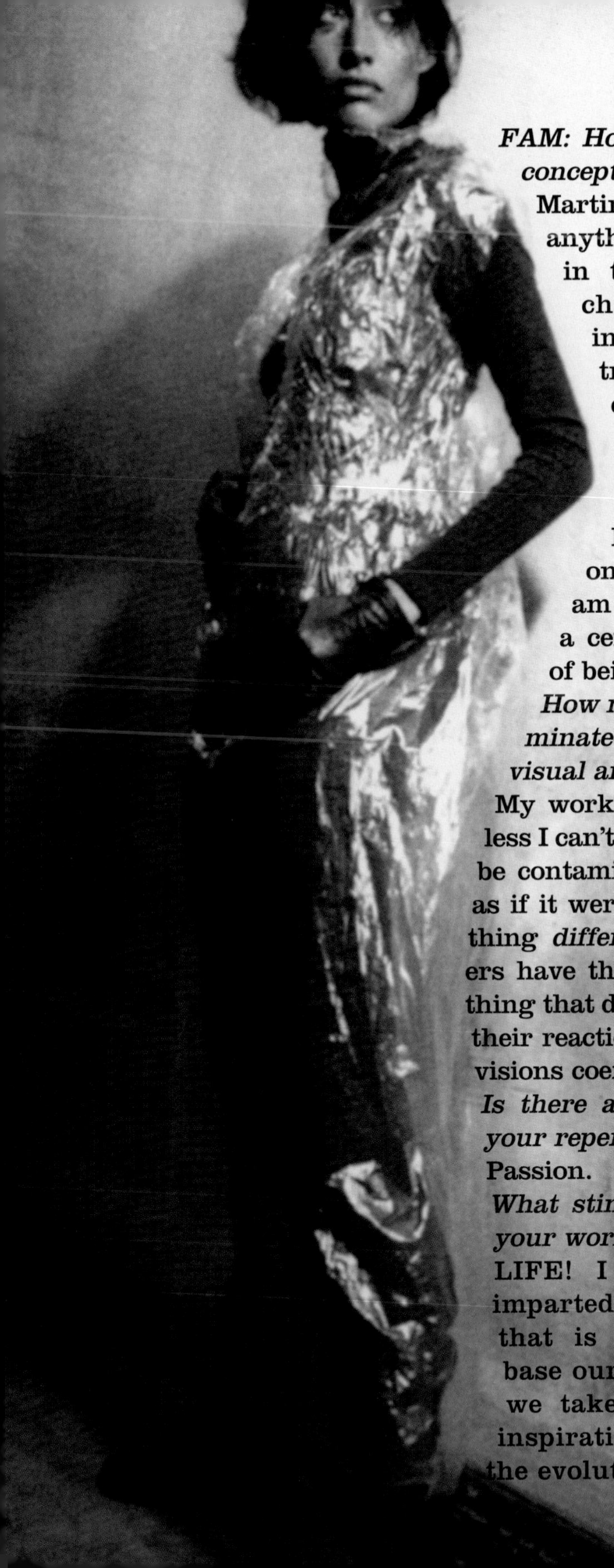

FAM: How would you define the concept of mutation?

Martin Margiela: More than anything else I am interested in the *spirit* of mutation: changing context and instead using the material transformation of an article as it is, for example, a shopping bag worn as a top.

What, for you, is the body?

More than concentrating on the form of the *body* I am interested in focusing on a certain behavior and state of being, mood.

How much is your work contaminated by imagery from the visual arts?

My work is visual, and nevertheless I can't see if it's possible for it to be contaminated by the visual arts as if it were contaminated by something *different*. Artists and designers have the same stimuli, the only thing that differs is the expression of their reaction to this stimulus; their visions coexist as parallels.

Is there a key word for defining your repertory?

Passion.

What stimulates you the most in your work?

LIFE! I think the education imparted to us gives us a *culture* that is ours, upon which we base ourselves, and from which we take our inspiration. This inspiration evolves along with the evolution of our background.

Winter 1992–1993. Photo Marina Faust

71

Winter 1994-1995. Photo Marina Faust

An encounter with David LaChapelle, the thirty-three-year-old New York photographer who calls his photographs "eye candy." His photographs are of bodies and images that already belong to spectacle, but are inserted directly in his multicolor imagery transforming and redefining them.

DAVID LACHAPELLE

interview by FRANCESCA ALFANO MIGLIETTI

Francesca Alfano Miglietti: How would you define yourself?
David LaChapelle: I take photographs to amuse myself, I don't try to take photographs for others. Photography is, for me, the way to do what I want; that's why, when people ask me things like, "What's your 'personal' work?" I answer that all of my work is personal. Ever since I was a kid I've always loved music and the pop art of Andy Warhol, who was the first artist I worked for (when I was seventeen years old); he taught me that one must not distinguish the famous personal "search" from everything else; and for me there's no difference between personal work and the work I do for advertising, my books, and what I use for newspapers. I always try to do what I like, because I don't believe that the quality of a work is its real finality. Who ever said that a photograph taken for a newspaper is different from one shown in a gallery? In my case they're the same thing, because in both cases I'm doing whatever it is I want. For example, photographing the Smashing Pumpkins with their families was a direct connection to my personal life, since I like their music a lot. I have no fixed mental compartments: personal work, commissioned work, or professional work are, for me, all exactly the same thing.
You reproduce amusing images, introducing an important artistic concept—visual fun. It's clear that you have fun when you work. What is art to you?
I think the most interesting and vital aspect of art is its state of continual change, and this is true also for its limits, which are never exactly defined. Someone can always come out and surprise you with something you've never considered art; that's why I think one of the aspects that distinguishes artists is their ability to be curious and never take the world and its limits as something set in stone. This is also true for photography. I follow the philosophy of Hiro, who said, "If you've already seen what you're seeing through the lens of your camera, don't take that photograph." Anyway, I think that there's creativity in each one of us, and that deep down every-

Smashed Glasses and Crystal, New York, 1994

one could be artists, if only they really wanted to . . .

What idiom do you feel most "contaminated" by?

I'm unable to follow a hard-and-fast separation between photography, cinema, music, and art . . . Perhaps filmmaking is one of the fields in which one can incorporate all of the other arts, and being a great director is the most powerful thing in art because you're able to collect all the disciplines into one. You can move people with music, the written word, acting, and visual power, and bring everything together . . . it's incredible.

Right now a lot of artists are working with the body: mutated, technological, modified bodies . . . Your bodies are sunny, festive, disorienting, pyrotechnic. What importance does the body have for you?

Many artists today are considering desperate, diseased, lost bodies . . . I think I'm rebelling against this inclination. Everything that immediately becomes mannered bothers me: even when I was little, and I wanted to become a painter, I painted the opposite of what everyone else was painting. Living in New York you're exposed to things like desperation and bewilderment on a daily basis, so I try to represent the exact opposite. My photographs are my way of escaping reality. They look to a period when sex was fun and you didn't have to watch out or be afraid, they deal with spontaneity and a certain joie de vivre . . . this is the fantasy I try to represent. Seeing these photographs some people say to me, "How can you present images like this, it's fake, the woman has breast implants," but for me it's something natural, it's a form of escape, it's mixing sexuality and humor, it's the return to a time in which sex was one of the joys of life! Substantially, my photos are an escape from what it really means to live in 1997 in New York, Milan, or Paris.

Chanel Diamond Brooch, Paris, 1995

Don't you think that, in that sense, art is a visionary drug?

Yes, but art is definitely the best drug . . . For example, during the Great Depression in America people were crazy about cinema, or musicals; even if they didn't have any money they spent every last penny to go see a film, to escape the heaviness all around them. They were starving for fantasy and imagination—that drug called art, music, fashion, and photography. The same thing is happening today with cinema, music, art; and many of my photographs, as I said, are also a particular form of escape, an escape from reality. I try to take a few things and transform them. I also think that in fashion right now something is coming up that one could call a "false reality," . . . for example, you take a model, you dress her up in a $900 dress and then you present her as if she died of starvation, penniless, scratching herself, really very depressed . . . but all that is false, because she's a model and because you put that type of dress on her. My photographs are much more honest, because they're fantasies and don't expect to be considered real. Because of this, I think, fashion magazines and photographers are through . . . Personally, I'm moving toward cinema.

So you're interested in images that are far from reality?

That's exactly what I want. I'm distancing myself from reality, from the monotony of an existence that's become a sort of blackmail: since life is sad, then also art and fashion and everything else have to be. I think you have to get used to doing what you want, to representing your own imagery, without any prudishness . . . It's those who force us to live a monotonous, boring life who should be ashamed, not those who free their

BARRYMORE

own fantasy like a rainbow. Substantially, I'm only creating my life and the way in which I want to live it, that's why I always work with friends and people I love. I like to surround myself with people who are a little crazy and very, very positive: it's really amazing to meet strange people from the whole world, and it's very important to be like them, have a child's soul . . . That's why I try not to ever use supermodels, and prefer to go and look for other girls who really want to do the photographs, who would give anything to do it. Their personality is fundamental, and I'm capable of capturing it in just a few minutes of conversation. My choice doesn't depend on the face, because any girl can become beautiful with the right makeup. What's really important in my photographs is finding a team of slightly crazy people who make the work like one big party.

Who are your favorite artists?
I could list infinite names: for example, I like a lot and am inspired by people like Fellini, De Sica, Gould, Andy Warhol, Pierre et Gilles, Jean-Paul Gaultier . . .

Do you think that the current art system, a system that continues to think only about the galleries and museums, is obsolete by now? Isn't it better to turn up the volume, don't you think, of what you have to say, rather than keeping an isolated "message" only for the chosen few?
I agree with you; I think galleries can become a major limitation. Sure, someone could say, for example in my case, "No, no, you're a fashion photographer, not an artist." This can really get you down, but I declare myself an artist and I don't care what people say about me; labels aren't important. I'm glad to have the chance to create. I'm glad to know that I'm an artist.

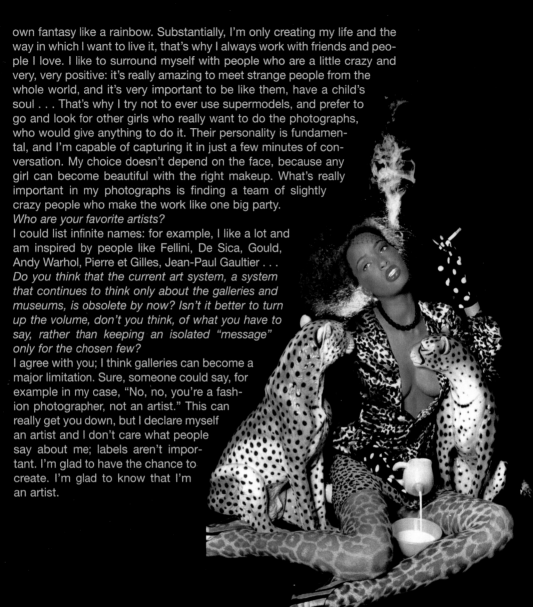

Brandi with Boob Cup and Ceramic Leopards, New York, 1995

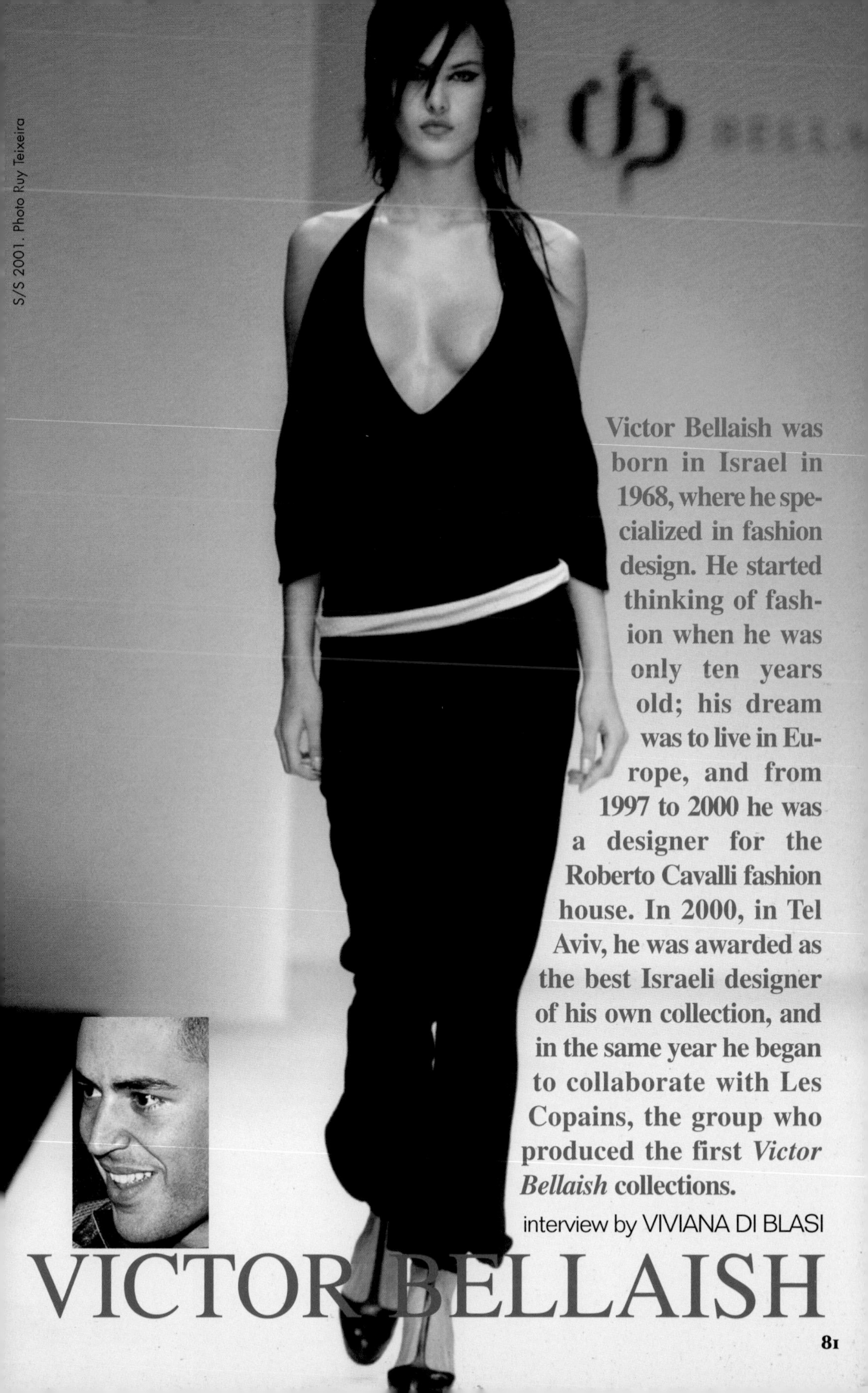

Victor Bellaish was born in Israel in 1968, where he specialized in fashion design. He started thinking of fashion when he was only ten years old; his dream was to live in Europe, and from 1997 to 2000 he was a designer for the Roberto Cavalli fashion house. In 2000, in Tel Aviv, he was awarded as the best Israeli designer of his own collection, and in the same year he began to collaborate with Les Copains, the group who produced the first *Victor Bellaish* collections.

interview by VIVIANA DI BLASI

VICTOR BELLAISH

81

Viviana Di Blasi: Jewish culture is perpetually nomadic as a consequence of numerous persecutions. How does being "Sabra" reflect itself in your current work?

Victor Bellaish: When I create my clothing I don't feel restricted by a traditional or conventional culture that imposes a certain way of designing, that always forces me back into its track, as the heir of other great designers. I create with my free spirit: I was born in a fairly young country, not yet crystallized, with a mix of backgrounds and different cultures that give me the privilege of engaging myself completely, in my creations, with an original level of design and style.

What are the most stimulating elements for you?

A cosmopolitan feeling—a crossroads between races, styles, and light tensions. I think that in the current climate it is possible to choose an "in color" or "black and white" life for oneself. I personally feel the need of color as an atmosphere in which to live, I love reds, flashy tones: the decision to exist, on the condition of existing in color!

Yours is a hybridization of different bodies, between the human and the mythological, between the past and the future, thus your figures are of women who are simultaneously aliens and sirens, cyborgs and medusas, warriors and sorceresses that walk the paths of a consciousness which negates them any single role.

I think that what distinguishes our time is the consciousness of a hybridization between culture, nature, technology, and the possibility of extending oneself beyond the canonical limits, both in fashion and one's own background. I personally feel I'm the son of an age that has no need of a strong culture of belonging, nor of a strong style with which one has to identify.

You move in a horizon in which the body and technology are constantly in relation, a horizon of globalized interfaces, of an artificiality that enters into the body and marks individuals' daily lives. Like an alchemist, you mix silicone and cashmere, silk and scales. . .

I've chosen the fluidity of a metamorphic identity. That's what woman is for me, I design for a woman who changes, who doesn't lock herself into the rigid style of the cultural need to belong—to a man, to a closed culture, to a determined period.

Fire and water: these are the drastic elements of an appearance that has no need for reservation; materials and skin enter into a relation where they play a layering game, making it difficult to distinguish.

What I want is to communicate passions, the devastating soul of a woman who doesn't live on the catwalk, but gets into a bus, in a chaotic and saturated metropolis in which after a few minutes the bus can explode!

The attention of fashion designers and artists is focused on the body: what role does the body have in your work?

In my collection *Kiss of the Spiderwoman* the body was put in high relief, silicone merged as an inseparable part of the body . . . The connection between clothing and body is the most important thing for me, there is a strong interaction, and adaptation to the feminine figure without interference or force. I think women love to be alive and appreciated for reaffirming themselves as women, for accentuating their own phenomenal character; fashion, on the other hand, doesn't follow this progression, it tends to underline the fatal or anorexic aspects, and I don't like that.

In what ways do you feel influenced by daily life?

S/S 2002

I am struck and moved by people, acquaintances, my closest friends, people's energy; they manage to touch me deeply, they can make me happy or sad, and my behavior moves along in step with my heart and the heart of the people. I like to be helpful, I'm sensitive to the needs and feelings of others, I observe and deepen situations, I take positions, get passionate, and go beyond.

What does woman, the figure of woman, represent for you?

I like it, I adore making clothes for women, men's clothing is less complicated or perhaps less liberal; I love the beauty that's behind women, women's bodies are intoxicating, pure creation, woman gives light to clothing, and fills it with her body, giving it life. That's why models are different. I could design a dress with superhuman effort, using materials and changing in continuation, but the spirit, body, and behavior of a woman are what manage to take the dress to the stars or turn it into a total failure.

Bare-Breasted
bodies exposed between fashion and rock

Thoracic cages pant on almost every stage—rock, pop, metal, punk, techno—charged with messages, made-up or tattooed, nude chests from both minimal stages and glam stages, at techno consoles . . . Symbol of rock and its idea of transgression, the bared breast paraded on the stage has invaded catwalks and fashion shows, penetrating music videos and haute couture as well. It maintains its charisma, unchanged, even if the trend leans toward uncovering always more modified, tattooed, mutated bodies.

by FAUSTO CALETTI

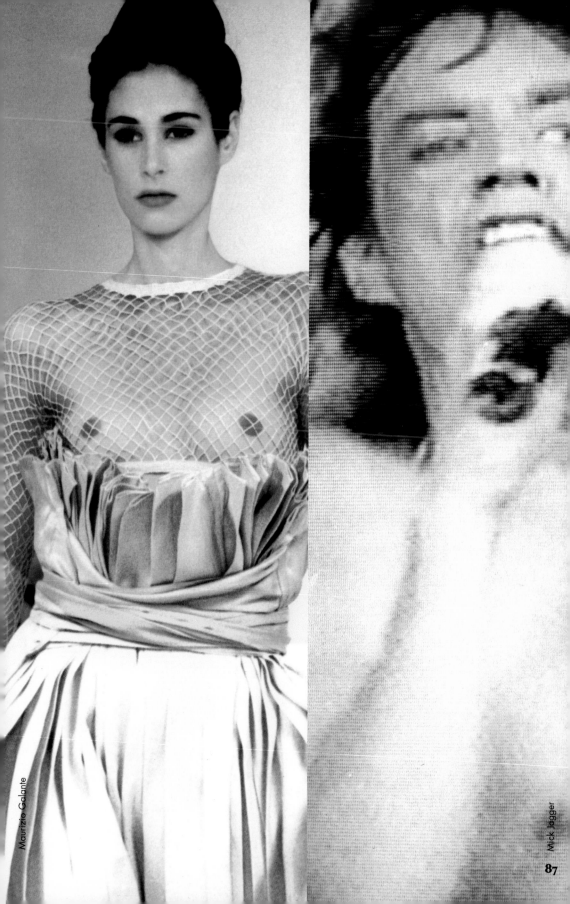

Maurizio Galante

Mick Jagger

John Richmond

Jean-Paul Gaultier

Givenchy

George Michael

John Galliano

89

Iggy Pop

Guns 'n Roses

Red Hot Chili Peppers

Betsey Johnson

Henry Rollins

Alexander McQueen

Antonio Berardi

The rock music of the 1970s was an ode to nudity, with Iggy Pop, Mick Jagger, and David Bowie: it was a sexy and wild nudity, which emphasized the subversive yearning of the times. They were years in which fashion had already digested the nude look of Yves Saint Laurent in 1967, the outfits of hippies, with all their transparencies, and above all miniskirts and hot pants. Then, in the 1980s, music stripped itself even further, with Billy Idol, Freddie Mercury, Prince, and George Michael in *I Want Your Sex*.

At the height of the 1980s the dramatic awakening to HIV caused a total shock and complete flip of earlier trends.

Rock and pop music got dressed again; fashion continues to be sexy and "peek-a-boo," but no longer offers a wholly nude look.

That was the apotheosis of *habillé* (dressed) exhibitionism, even if it remained a deceit of censors. Even Madonna, who often played with nudity when she was explicit, has always made moderated use of it, as one would expect of a self-assured diva.

Marilyn Manson

Freddie Mercury

In the minimalism of the 1990s nudity clearly triumphed in fashion. Music assumed different values, and no longer felt the need to strip. The early 1990s were characterized by a design that accentuated the decorative use of the body as suggested by the splendid creations of Ferré, Versace, and Vivienne Westwood.

After that everything changed, the profound socio-economic crisis put, once and for all, a minimalist taste at the top of fashion.

The body no longer has a physical value, but becomes smooth, eccentric, hairless, forever young, and completely cerebral. People view an exhibited body as a container of cerebral concepts, a body almost without materiality.

Designers create diaphanous outfits, as if the clothes were under the skin, using artificial films made of synthetic fibers.

In the new fashion the taste for the nude and crude "real life" has ceased to give a sexy view of the human nude, because the bodies it

Ann Demeulemeester

Vivienne Westwood

Dell'Acqua

Sonia Rikiel

Jim Morrison

93

shows have nothing carnal about them. Nude bodies and skin offer no more than an alternative to clothes. Anorexia has become a fashion, creating a practically interchangeable idea of masculine and feminine esthetics. While over the course of the last decade rock music got dressed, fashion and its communication got naked, in a stripped-down search for new expressions that are closer to the life of the common mortal; what could be closer to us than our own skin?

Walter van Beirendonck

Gucci

Dirk Bikkembergs

Walter van Beirendonck

D&G

Prince

95

Jean-Paul GAULTIER

Curious, witty, irreverent, transgressive, exuberant . . . an encounter with Jean-Paul Gaultier, one of the most unpredictable and brilliant creators of fashion.

interview by FAM

FAM: Virus is a magazine of contaminations, and your way of working is also full of contaminations. What, for you, is contamination?

Jean-Paul Gaultier: Contamination, for me, is an opening; it's being open to transformations, to that which mutates. I think I'm someone who "eats" a lot: for me contamination is like eating, I eat everything and afterwards I digest. I assimilate all sorts of things, countries, cultures, people of different social classes, people on the street, daytime people, night owls. I absorb everything and I like lots of things, I don't set up barriers, things can be completely different, and the more different they are the more I like them, the more they interest me. And it's the same with music, words, language, images, traditions; I absorb everything, in a permanent contamination . . .

Right now people can choose their own identities; they can intervene on their own bodies to modify and determine their own identities. Do you ever think of these bodies when you design?

Yes, quite often. The idea of the body is the basis of my work, and it's not a still life, but something that lives; for me the body is structure, an architectural base. The inside and outside of the body interest me, and I think about this also as I look for articles to work with. Actually, I'm convinced that even the inside of a body must be beautiful, because that's what is in contact with the skin . . . It's an obsession, a combination, an overlapping . . . like the relationship between the identity of the garment I make and that of the body wearing it. For me, a garment is a second skin—on occasion I've made very light, transparent pieces printed like tattoos . . .

Do you think there are still distinct masculine and feminine identities that

Photo Pierre Vauthey

remain immutable over time, or that there is transformation and interaction between the two?

I think that people change, and that their identities change as well; think of clothes—one communicates through dress. A person's mood can change from morning to evening, and this changes his identity. Identity, for me, changes from one minute to the next, from one day to the other, and it's a form of evolution. That's what I find interesting in clothes as well, and it's what I try to express in every garment I make.

But don't you think that both a masculine and feminine identity can live within the same person?

Yes, I think that we're all men and women made of a sensibility that can be male for women and female for men. It's the way we're brought up that has separated this complementarity. Usually only a part of the man and a part of the woman shows itself, even if the slightly masculine woman has never been considered a real taboo, while an effeminate man has always been viewed very negatively. That's the banality and "condemnation" of the virile man, with all his "power" and all his "duty." Looking at the details of masculine bodies, for example, you can ascertain a conformist and scandalous mentality: do you know why men's jackets button from left to right, the opposite of women's jackets? Because that way you can easily stick your hand in to get your wallet and pay! This has a social significance in terms of role, belonging to a certain role, a declaration of inferiority or superiority. I find these distinctions scandalous, even if in the last few years man—the concept of man—has changed a lot. Man's view of himself has changed, as has women's view of man. Today it's plausible that a man is no longer forced to play the theatrical role of virility, and that he's able to show his sensitivity. For years men's sensitivity was censored, because society required that men not show their own emotions. I think that this new sensitivity, which is finally being shown by men, is also a new form of seduction.

Transgender, transitory, mixed, and reversible identities; given all these, isn't it limiting to think of a collection for men and a separate one for women?

Certainly—in fact, for me, everything has always been mixed; but there are still a lot of antiquated rules in the fashion world . . . Don't you think it's stupid that on an organizational level there are different dates for the presentation of the women's collection and the men's? Spring arrives at the same time for everyone! It's like building a restaurant for men and a separate one for women . . . I find it ridiculous to divide the world according to sex, and that naturally goes for fabrics as well; for me sex exists neither in fabrics nor in garments' forms. A men's skirt, for example—why not? For me this has nothing to do with cross-dressing; I think cross-dressing happens when the body of a man is dressed in elements that typically belong to a woman's body, and vice versa, like a bra, for example . . . But even this is changing, as you well know there are a lot of people working to modify their own bodies, men who decide to have a womanly bust without becoming "women" just because of that! Today it's possible to be completely male but choose to have a beautiful bust . . . and if with a nice breast one feels more beautiful, why not? We're moving in this direction, toward this type of conscious mutation.

In the near future might you design bodies instead of clothing?

That's an idea! I think the most significant thing at the moment is the transformation that people decide to undergo with their own bodies . . . Think of plastic surgery, which at first was done only after an accident or for a disease; now it's an instrument of transformation, and the same is true of tattooing and piercing. I find the idea of using one's own body as a sculpture to be decorated or transformed, or in any case modified, very new. Thus the body can become a work of art, one's own work of art. All this is very fascinating, and above all much more radical than clothing, because it's definitive and completely belongs to one's life; it's like an act of love, a very romantic way of saying I want myself for the rest of my life, and from that point of view you can do anything, starting off here to try out new types of skin. I find all that truly fascinating, as well as the idea of working with identity, that which really matches us or which we'd like, what we'd like to be, the possibility of recognizing oneself in another body . . . all this has already begun with transsexuals.

How do you define yourself?

I'll tell you right away that I don't think of myself as an artist, but rather as someone who makes clothing, and I have a true passion for it. I began practicing this trade thanks to my grandmother. My grandmother was a nurse and had a personal clientele, and for these patients she administered not only shots but also therapeutic massages, and beauty massages as well. She also earned their complete trust and gave them advice on how to dress, changing hairstyles, and cooking recipes. And I, a seven-year-old, listened in. The interesting thing is that by the age of seven I already knew all the private and sentimental affairs of these women, and I drew them as they were and how I imagined they could be. My imagination was a little restricted, and was tied to the models of seduction that I had seen on television, the actresses . . . What my grandmother's way of life taught me was really the importance of how one presents oneself, the fact that your way of presenting yourself becomes your way of communicating, the importance of how a dress or haircut can say something about you . . . This is what interests me in fashion: the people interest me more than the garments, and the invention of ways of communicating one's own identity.

Who are your favorite fashion designers?

Margiela and Comme des Garçons. The thing I find incredible about Comme des Garçons is that the fashion designer is a woman, and she's who designs; and when women make fashion they really have a strength that men don't have. It's a sort of vis-à-vis between women, a social metamorphosis . . . One thing that I've always found shocking and absurd, and totally without a real reason, is the discrimination between men and women, a discrimination that regards salaries as well: in many trades and fields, for the same function, a woman is paid less than a man. Paradoxically, the profession of being a supermodel is the only one where the opposite is true, which proves the fact that in this line of work a woman is recognized not for her value or her abilities and talents, but for her exterior and superficial aspect.

What is the artistic medium that most contaminates your creativity?

I would say video and cinema, because I like spectacle a lot, and fashion is also a spectacle, with its shows. My first grand, true emotion was when I first went to the theater with my grandmother to see an operetta—I found that world marvelous. I still like the part of spectacle that there is in fash-

ion a lot, and it's my reason for always presenting my fashion shows in an extremely spectacular way.

Virus is dealing with an extreme art made up of things that mutate. Does this very radical aspect of art interest you?

Very much—I find it particularly interesting, because you do it with your own flesh, which is the most essential thing that we have. In London I witnessed some performances by Franko B and Ron Athey: I was also very fascinated and disquieted by the way this art was presented, the scenography, the gestural nature, the way of intertwining the different idioms with flesh and blood. It's exceptional. The human body interests me very much, and therefore these art forms do as well. I think performances of this type are quite different from those of the 1960s, because they are able to intermingle the most advanced technologies with tribal rituals, one's own desire to modify himself with the possibilities of extending corporeal limits. I am interested in the same way by virtual representations, holograms, and the robotic dimension; I think that very soon there could be half-holographic and half-robotic, half-robotic and half-human, half-holographic and half-human "beings."

We've talked a lot about contamination between idioms, beings, and identities; how do you see the contamination between the world's North and South in the near future—as a symbiosis or a conflict?

I believe that in the near future the conflicts will move to colonies outside the world, because in the world we're learning to live together . . . Finally people travel, mix, and reproduce in mixed races. There will still be ethnic conflicts, but they'll always be rarer, until the point when humanity will be completely mixed and wars will take place on other planets. People will enlarge their own cultural fabric with trips, cuisine, and clothing. And now the phenomenon of contamination is also happening between religions: there are a lot of people who are starting to construct their own religion by mixing elements of Buddhism, Christianity, and Islam; on his own, man is beginning to construct his own religion, and is doing so because he travels and sees and gets to know other ways of living, of relating to oneself and everything. Think, for example, of cuisine: currently in Paris alone there are seventy Japanese restaurants, and think of pizza's invasion throughout the entire world!

Jamaican by birth and "scholastically educated" in America, Jessica Ogden moved to London, where she attended art school for three years. Here are the sculpture- and painting-like dresses, and a showroom constructed like an installation, of who is now considered one of the most fascinating fashion designers of London.

interview by FRANKO B

JESSICA OGDEN

Franko B: I'd like to ask you some very simple things, like where you were born and when and why you arrived in London.
Jessica Ogden: I was born in Jamaica, grew up there, and went to school in America, where I began college; but then I understood that it wasn't where I wanted to stay, so I moved to London, fundamentally seeking out a freedom that I hadn't found in America. For three years in London I attended a college where I principally worked with photographs of women. But when I left I wanted to work more closely with people.
More closely in what sense?
In a certain way I wanted to return to how I had originally considered individuals, in other words, basing my view on their personality more than how fashion considers them. Actually I'm working in fashion because I'm trying to transmit sensations to the people who wear my clothes; but not all of my models are wearable, some are works of art.
What is a work of art and what isn't?
I think that consumerism is what makes this distinction; a distinction that I don't make because I'm trying to work without any type of restriction, thinking that everything I do is art.
How do you view the bond between the clothes you make and the body (aside, obviously, from the fact that being worn is usually the principal function of clothing)?
I work outside of and on the body. I try to find a balance between some dresses that are for the body and others that are instead against the body. Sometimes I make dresses that ruin the body so completely that I'd like to toss them out the window; in a certain sense it's a way to create a new form for the body.
Do you consider your dresses a second skin or simply as dresses?
I always try to see them as sculptures; in theory they are linked to

the human body, but my mental process is fairly egotistical because I always see my clothes as an end in themselves. In a certain sense I don't think of them as being for the body. What I mean to say is that the contradiction that characterizes them is that on the one hand they're just something you wear, and therefore become a part of your body, while on the other hand they are an excerpt of my creative process.

Last year in London you had an exhibition of your clothing that seemed more like a show of sculptures or paintings; it didn't matter to you whether someone would ever wear them. As I look at the photographs of your showroom I find it looks a lot like the installation work you did years ago. So, what are the differences, if there are any, between the past and the present?

I think that work is a continual progression; I'm not in the fashion world to just do two collections a year, but rather to express my art.

What caused you to use for your clothes materials and objects that were already used by other artists in their performances?

When it came to my mind to use your bed sheets, what prompted me was the fact that it was a matter of the process having been the start of your performance: it wasn't a remainder, but a product, and it was a piece of pure fabric, perhaps the purest that I could find in connection to something that has happened.

We're talking about pieces of fabric that I used during a performance in which I lose blood and lie on the ground in a sort of martyrdom: you were able to make use of it for your work because you knew in what way it had been used.

Yes, as I already said it was the product of your work, and with that I was able to add realism to my dress, since nothing more real than that could be found: it was the blood of Franko B that had left those signs. Regarding the approach to these pieces of fabric, at first I think that it's not my blood, it's not totally my product, it's a part of Franko that he permitted me to use to make it become what I wanted. But then I ask myself other questions: how can I touch this blood that isn't mine? And in circumstances like this infantile fears like "stay away from blood" come back to mind . . . But I try to fight my own prejudices and I tell myself, "no, I want to penetrate this piece of fabric and make it become my own because the work of Franko B is very important to me." For me Franko is worth so much as a person that I refuse to be afraid of his blood; above all what causes me to open up to this piece of fabric is the trust that Franko demonstrated by allowing me to make what I wanted with a piece of his work. To thank you for your trust I convince myself not to be afraid of these sheets.

Do you think you know the sort of people who like your work? Do you believe that they are different from those who follow Franko B, Ron Athey, or Annie Sprinkle?

I think that there is a continuous remixing among those who follow my work, but not among those who buy it. One of my wishes is to succeed in producing dresses to buy, in such a way that they can truly be appreciated.

Do you believe you've finished your mutations?

I don't know; there are pieces that after five years have changed,

S/S 2001. Photo Amber Rolands

they've become different depending on whether they've been with other people or with me. This is because they are part of a process in which I make something exist and then I let it change automatically.

Some people talk about technology and consider the body something obsolete, while others don't see it this way. How do you balance these two positions? Do you think there's one single way of considering the issue, or do you see also a process of mutation in the human race and its thoughts?

There are various aspects. On the one hand I am quite obsolete myself: I stay in studio by myself . . . but this isn't my unique nature, it's one of many. We're all changing, it's like a group of people that are moving; if you want to change something you can fight for years without reaching your target, while as an artist you can get directly to the point by representing whatever you want.

By the age of twenty-seven you've already worked for important people who consider you very promising: for example, they're comparing you to Alexander McQueen. How does this judgment influence your work?

It's something you can't control, so I don't worry about people's judgment: whatever comes to you, you have to make it come out. My goal isn't to attain success, but rather to continue doing what I'm doing, which is something I feel very tied to. Certainly, in the past this caused me a lot of problems because what I did wasn't "in style." So I had to find a way to continue earning a living staying honest to myself.

You also can't repeat your works because you often work with material derived from the work of other artists. How do you view this collaboration?

I absolutely want to continue with it because it allows me to express what I think of the people I work with. Sometimes I have feelings I'm unable to put into words. But when I send an artist a work of mine made from a piece of theirs, then I manage to talk, even without words.

First political dispute, then chains, metal bosses, and the black leather dresses that invented punk. Today, crinolines, lace bodices, and historical references. Here is a creator of fashion with the courage of authenticity.

Vivienne Westwood

by MICHELE CIAVARELLA

The queen of fashion has red hair. Her face is pale, her stride elegant—that of a true gentlewoman. She's imperious atop her platform shoes, but her majestic walk is winged, without gravity. It is with the same lightness that Vivienne Westwood has gone from playing the role of the extremists' heroine to that of the "most influential creator of fashion in the second half of this century," as John Fairchild, editor of *Women's Wear Daily*, the only daily fashion newspaper, described her in 1989. Indeed, the most influential and the most copied. Her crinnies, the revised and corrected seventeenth-century crinolines, her rubber dresses, her ultra-high platform shoes, and her bras worn on top of the dresses have been copied by all the most famous and high-praising colleagues of the fashion business system. She's not much interested in being copied, and it may bore her even more to be defined "the mother of all fashion designers."

"If they copy me, my prestige increases. It means I'm good. But it also disappoints me a bit, because copies are always uglier than the originals," says Queen Viv. This is the calm, balanced reaction of one who is used to inventing movements that then become the patrimony of entire generations. Even before fashion, Vivienne was already the queen of punk when in London it was common to spit on the crown. She came from a world that seemed to come straight out of a Ken Loach film script, made of unemployment, poverty, and food stamps.

Vivienne Isabel Swire was born April 8, 1941, in a small village in Derbyshire to a family of textile workers. Her mother named her after the actress Vivienne Leigh. She arrived in London with her parents, when she was seventeen years old. She was already a young schoolteacher when she met Malcom McLaren, leader of the Sex Pistols, and became his partner, muse, and accomplice. "We didn't respect the hypocritical politics of the period," she tells, "and we wanted to upset the English. We wanted to bother them. Sex and the representation of violence allowed us to get immediate results." Almost unhoped-for results, perhaps. Two detonators had met . . . McLaren opened up the road to a new life, far from her first marriage to Mister Westwood, which had quickly soured. Vivienne left teaching, changed her flower-child look, cut her hair back to shaggy tufts, and started selling jewelry at Portobello Road Market. In 1968 she became the mother of Joseph Ferdinand (who now has a sexy lingerie shop in Soho) and became ever more determined in her mission as a de-stabilizer. In 1971 this volcano of projects gets an outlet with the opening of Let it Rock, a boutique where black leather jackets, bossed sweaters, and teddy boy clothes are sold. Each year Vivienne and Malcom change the name and atmosphere of the shop, until in 1974 the age of Sex arrives, a point of no return: rubber clothes, leather and vinyl accessories, chains and t-shirts with the slogans "Only anarchists are pretty," "Anarchy is melody," and "Modernity kills every night." The police shut down the store, exasperated by the anarchic mottos more than anything else. It did no good. The place was about to be rechristened "Seditionaries" to give a recipe to the furor and revolt of the 1970s. And while McLaren was founding the Sex Pistols, she designed clothing beyond all measure; "challenging clothing," as she defines it today. "Her place" at 430 King's Road changed name again and became World's End (it's still today one of the most curious attractions of London, with its large clock that vertiginously signals the hour backwards).

Time passes quickly. In Great Britain the battleaxe Thatcher arrives on the scene, and the punk phenomenon is slowly diluted by the complications of the 1980s. But Vivienne still designs clothes, and in 1981 organizes her first fashion show at London's Olympia: the collection is called *Pirate* and is inspired by the outlaws of all periods throughout history. In 1983 she is invited to present a fashion show in Paris, and is the first English fashion designer, after Mary Quant, to get such results. The following year she breaks up the emotional and artistic union with McLaren and many people wonder if the time has arrived for even the fashion designer to quit. But it's not. In Paris her crinnies cause an uproar. But why, she asks. "Clothing has always reconstructed and modified the architecture of the body, even if today it seems to be forbidden to do so. To design a dress with a sellier, the padding that gives it a round form, has become a subversive act. In a time of democratic prejudices, everything must be submitted for approval, checked, and contained within precise limits. Yesterday

no one cared about people's prejudices, and today public opinion is tighter than a straitjacket."

Not that this prevents her from offering, from that moment on, only what she likes. And what she likes after the end of punk merges with the immense inheritance of historic references that can live together with the present. "Through fashion I try to re-evoke the past and reflect on it. With respect to today, the past had a society of elite as a model of reference—privileged people who reached the highest apex of quality and refinement, supporting art and culture. Certainly, they were also snobs, intellectuals who believed in the importance of appearance. In the last century there was a false belief that with scientific progress there would be opportunities for all and the world would come to resemble paradise. That's not how it went. If one doesn't consider the past, great technical resources are lost, as is the possibility to manipulate materials, which are the heart of fashion. My technique is precisely that of inserting and translating the knowledge of the past into the mass production of the present."

Thus the Westwood style was born, which upsets the certainties upon which all creators of fashion rely. And in fashion there are infusions of culture, which Vivienne brings to life from the novels of Flaubert and the essays of social criticism by Bertrand Russell. All this, in the 1980s, has the same shocking impact that the underground movements had in the

previous decade. Her approach to the establishment also changes: "Once I used to attack it and I didn't realize that I was playing along with its game, because in order to live the establishment always needs an opposition. Today I ignore it and focus my attention on more important things: history, civilization, the relationship between conformity of ideas and the uniformity of dress. And even between orthodoxy and heresy: the former is the death of intelligence."

1987 Collection. Photo Kim Knott

These meanings that infuse her clothing certainly don't get to the broader public, but they do shock her colleagues and win over fashion critics. Vivienne Westwood becomes the point of reference. The schools and universities where fashion and costuming courses have been put into place call her to teach classes. Paris, the home of international fashion, ideas, and, up to that point, business, wants to have regular fashion shows of her collections, and she becomes the most beloved of all those who work in the field and who recognize her great ability to give birth to ideas. From one success to another, even in Great Britain she becomes an important woman. By 1984 *Tatler*, London's snobby monthly magazine, portrays her with her platinum locks and a string of pearls round her neck, and in the style of the scandal-ridden tabloids cries, "This woman was punk."

Within the system, but outside of the system, Vivienne Westwood becomes the paragon of all that is alternative. The collections repeat with equal amounts of success and scandal. Finally, in 1990, she decides to apply her ideas to men's fashion as well, and in Florence sends her first entirely male collection out on the catwalk. As usual, it's a scandal . . .

But then, inevitably, her ideas are taken up by others; diluted and bent to meet the rules of marketing, they gain greater commercial success, as regularly happens also with the women's collections. It doesn't matter to her. In the same year she opens a store in the chic Mayfair section of London, at 6 Davies Street, and continues to nurture the extravagances of World's End. In 1992 she rises as far as Buckingham Palace to receive the OBE (Order of British Empire) from Elizabeth II. But she's not a tamed woman; at the exit the photographers insist that she twirl her long and ample skirt. The photoreporters' indiscreet lenses capture and document her hatred of underwear (which she never wears because the ones she wore as a child gave were a horrendous nuisance). Yet another scandal—she's insulted the queen. "That wasn't my intention," she angelically answers. "I have completely different opinions about the monarchy now than the anti-establishment ones that filled me at the time of the Sex Pistols. I find that an authentic aristocracy is much better than the one produced by Hollywood and TV."

No regrets, Vivienne doesn't deny. She has only the strength of authenticity, the same one that causes her to remark, about her fashion, "I hope that people understand that it's an allusion. I recall that a certain type of elegance passes through forms that we've since forgotten. Certain moments in history have a value that even today can illuminate us." Today the fashion of Vivienne Westwood is divided between two women's collections, *Gold Label* and *Red Label*, a men's collection, and the latest arrival, *Anglomania*, a collection uniting rebellion, fantasy, romanticism, and glamour in the purest English style. And who knows whether her perfume, which is about to be launched won't contain a bit of her spirit that can be summed up in one word—unique?

F/W 1996. Photo Inez Van Lamsweerde / Vinoodh Matadin, 1996

Matt Lehitka is the young German fashion designer who became famous in the fashion world when he debuted as a designer with the house of Christian Dior. Beyond his work with Dior he creates his own line, known as *Street Night Wear*. Matt also takes care of the management and promotion of Street Voice, an agency for international art and entertainment very active in New York and Cologne.

interview by
FLORENCE LYNCH

Matt Lehitka

Florence Lynch: How do you view your two activities, working for the Maison Dior and for Matt Lehitka?

Matt Lehitka: They're not so different. The ideas are mine, but obviously it's very important for me to work with other people, and that they accept my ideas; that's how it works with Groose. At the same time it's important that I work for myself, for my line, my projects, and so on. What's most important is that the collections, be they mine or Dior's, be free, high quality, and presented with professionalism.

Please tell me a bit about your design career prior to Dior.

I began to be interested in fashion when I was fifteen years old. My mother also worked in fashion, in haute couture. My interest in clothing began with her. She designed for me and I didn't like what she made. I cultivated my interest in fashion, and she helped me break into the profession. When I turned nineteen I matriculated in a fashion school in Düsseldorf; I stayed a year and then left for Paris, where I collaborated as a freelancer with various designers.

Why merging music and fashion was so important to you?

Music, for me, is an important means for being able to express myself clearly.

More precisely, is it fashion that you mix with the music, or the movement of the body?

When I speak of interaction with the music I mean that it's important for me to create connections between the various aspects that together make up a fashion project: and music is fundamental. When they are shown on the catwalk, my clothes are accompanied only by a submissive music, a light percussion or other instrument with hushed sonorities. My program is

related to space, it's not simply a fashion event. It's entertainment. The first part is fashion, the second is light, and, most importantly, the third is music. This is my way of presenting fashion. It's visual power: seeing, listening, and feeling. From 1990 to 1995, on the other hand, I worked on my fashion collection, created for other companies, and worked on the successful *WHA* line, in collaboration with a painter.

Was that your first collaboration in an artistic field? I know that you also work as an artist.

Yes, that was the first time I exposed myself and risked with art. Since then I've continued to collaborate on a musical entitled *Head to Head*, with great success. It was played in the theater district of Cologne with the participation of two Broadway actors, Ron White and Ron Talton.

What, according to you, is the relationship between your creation and the final buyer?

My creation, for now, is an idea: *Street Night Wear*. I want to prove that the garments I designed can be worn with other creations. When the buyer gets a garment from me, it can be paired with something he already has to create a new look. Mixing and matching is the idea behind *Street Night*

Wear. Almost everyone says it's street fashion; it's not street fashion, but rather an unseen conceptual configuration of fashion.

I'd like you to talk a little bit about your projects in the realm of art. You've shown in art galleries throughout Europe; why did you choose to wed fashion and art?

Art has great importance for me, and I consider it in a certain sense an entity unto itself. First comes art, then design. Art means the vanguard, it means being a precursor, it has a preponderant role in my creative process. It's like music. It has a strong influence on me, on my fashion, and on my way of thinking. That's why it's so important. There are numerous artists who have given me infinite emotions and the possibility of understanding many things. They gave me faith in what I do. Art is like Street Voice: it gives me very real impressions.

Naoki Takizawa. Photo Platon

Issey Miyake. Photo Tyen

NAOKI TAKIZAWA

In a rare—if not singular—gesture, Issey Miyake chose to entrust him with the full responsibility for the men's line that bears his name. It is truly rare that one who designs the collection has his name appear next to that of the "Master."
interview by FRANCA SONCINI

ISSEY MIYAKE, born in Hiroshima, with an international upbringing and mixed cultural background, is considered one of the masters of avant-garde fashion. His clothes, fruit of an admirable experimentation with materials and techniques, are bona fide artistic creations, autonomous objects free of all impediments and rigidities, in full harmony with, and modifying the form and meaning of, the body wearing them. In 1970 he founded the Miyake Design Studio, an extraordinary structure that gives many designers of different sensibilities and experiences the chance to express themselves and grow by working on collections and designs of various natures.
NAOKI TAKIZAWA, born in Tokyo in 1964, graduated from the Kuwasawa Design School in 1981, and in the following year began working at the Miyake Design Studio. Initially he was responsible for the *Plantation* line, in 1989 he began to work on the women's collection, and three years later he became an associate designer. In 1993, in confirmation of the respect granted him, Issey Miyake decided to entrust him with the full responsibility for the men's line named after him—a gesture that is rare, if not unique, for Miyake. It is truly rare that one who designs the collection has his name appear next to that of the "Master."

Franca Soncini: When you design a collection do you think of what you would like to have and wear?

Naoki Takizawa: No. When I design I don't think about making clothing for myself or that I will be the one to wear it; but when the collection is complete, then I do think about what I myself would wear. This way the creativity is fresher and one also has a lot more fun.

When you sit down to work on a collection, where do you start— materials, forms, or a concept? Do you always follow the same procedure or do you change your creative technique from one time to the next?

One begins with research, for example on fabrics, sewing techniques, and so on. I never begin with one thing in particular. The act of researching, of whatever type it might be, always leads me to the next step.

In each profession there is a pleasant side and others that are less stimulating; is there a phase of your work that you often find difficult or that you do more out of obligation than for your own pleasure?

Thinking about all that is classic; this proves how much more the future interests me.

Up to what point is the sense of duty important for your life, and to what point, on the other hand, do you follow your desires?

Duty is important, but following one's own wishes is equally so.

What are your creative roots?

The aspiration to always change the contingent situations.

Modern Japan is a mixture of excess and beauty. What most strikes you about that?

The essence of simplicity elegantly dressed in an intricate work has a strong tie with Japanese beauty. And sometimes it can be a source of ambiguity in the Japanese character.

You have worked for both men's and women's collections; do you find creating clothes for men and women very different, or are the objectives the same?

Designing for men is the creation of reality. Designing for women is the creation of fantasy.

Do you think that there is still a male identity and a female identity, or do the two extremes meet and almost cancel each other out?

I don't think that there is one single trend. It is chaos.

What do you maintain are the principal obstacles that one comes across in the fashion world? What do you wish were different?

The rules and traditional theories of the past. I like it when by wearing my clothes people feel freed.

What significance does modernity have for you? How and up to what point can technology transform our lives?

A society that gives any- and everyone the total freedom to learn. Hasn't your life changed in the past ten years? Think of computers, cellular phones, CD players and so on.

What value do esthetics have for you? In what terms would you describe your concept of beauty?

It is not easy to describe beauty with few words, but for me a psychological feeling is the essence of beauty.

What artistic styles have most influenced your creativity?

It doesn't necessarily have to be something artistic or beautiful. It is all that happens around us.

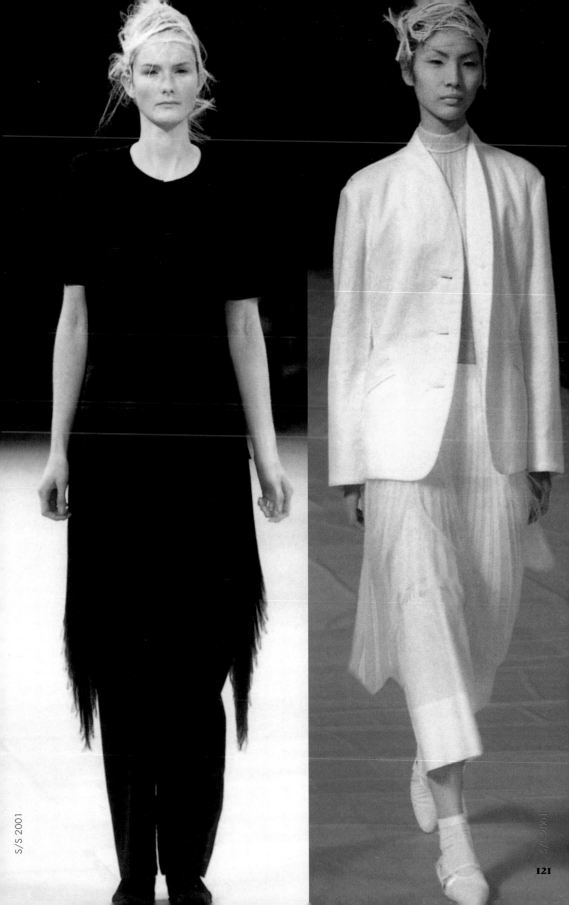

S/S 1999. Courtesy of Franca Soncini

You often use the term design, as if "fashion" didn't interest you; what value does the word "design" hold for you?

My interest in design is founded on materials and technology.

Your first show was in Milan; what motives led you to this decision? How was your first encounter with the city and its people? Was it an experience you hope to repeat?

I am firmly convinced that Milan is a city in which one can share his ideas wth others, thanks to its artisanal and entrepreneurial gifts. In Milan I would like to obtain high levels of quality paired with style. The people are warm, passionate, and perspicacious. I was struck, when working with them, at how they are able to concentrate on work and at the same time enjoy life.

S/S 1999. Courtesy of Franca Soncini

S/S 1999. Courtesy of Franca Soncini

Costume National

Passions and forecasts of the near future with Ennio Capasa,
one of the most interesting international fashion designers.

Ennio Capasa. Photo Joe Magrean

F/W 1998–1999. Photo Dino Scrimali

interview by
FRANCESCA ALFANO MIGLIETTI

FAM: You are part of a new generation of fashion designers. Are there different ways of interpreting fashion in the contemporary universe?
Ennio Capasa: My generation has worked hard to break into spaces that had grown restricted, saturated; and this, it seems to me, has brought a

Winter 2000–2001. Photo Manuel Vason

new authenticity to life. I believe the more spaces are restricted, the more necessary authenticity becomes. Today one no longer designs to create an "image," and we are witnessing the passage between fashion and style.
But what is fashion?
I think that the concept of fashion changes with the passing of time; what was fashion ten years ago no longer is. For me fashion, the healthy kind, the kind that interests me, represents contemporaneity, feeling in harmony with the moment in which one lives; this is what I struggle for—to understand my time through costume. The fashion that I design is made up of a sort of combinations that try to suggest an individual freedom, certainly not "uni-

Winter 2000–2001 . Photo Manuel Vason

forms" in which to uncritically hide. The possibility of helping to build an image through free combinations that relate themselves to individual personalities interests me. Up until now fashion has been almost a dictatorial, vertex-oriented structure, but luckily today people are much less willing to submit to the "orders" of fashion, and this is very interesting.

How did you start out?

In a strange way; I am not a fashion designer by vocation, and when I was a kid I never thought about becoming a fashion designer. For a series of adventurous reasons I found myself, almost unwittingly, working, in Japan, with a person as extraordinary as Yohji Yamamoto. His anomalous way of thinking about fashion seduced me; it was a collection of views of people of the street. The way of thinking of the body in Japan is the complete opposite of my own; they think of a body as an almost geometric structure, while I, who was born in Lecce and have always felt the attraction of the beauty of Magna Graecia, see in the body a fascinating place of individuality. Nevertheless, this ability to look to the creativity of the street really struck me; I can say that my work is a sort of alchemy between these two moments, a mix between high-level tailoring and the street, between the search for a formal harmony and the transgression of the street.

In the future you predict . . .

We're in a new century . . . when I was a kid the year 2000 seemed a faraway date, a dream . . . also because in the 1970s, when I was born, 2000 was a sort of myth, with NASA, space voyages . . . it was the passage into another era. The future is perhaps less scenographic but certainly as intense, perhaps more so, than one could imagine. The changes are truly profound, and everything is being radically modified. Western civilization has had three moments of strong change: that of Greek Hellenism, that of the Renaissance—which laid the foundations for a whole series of discussions of modernity—and the contemporary one, a change of civilization, an amplified vision, a transformation of the entire planet, a transformation that ranges from flavors to consciences . . . We are changing in our beds.

What do you mean by an amplified vision?

A lack of awareness has often limited human potential. Frequently we have no idea of the possibilities we have to transform ourselves, to "become." The concept of becoming unfolds partially in art, in theater, in cinema; but a more attentive culture in this sense could prove that each individual could aspire to this type of transformation, aspire to a more creative society. Primitive societies are in this sense very indicative, because they reveal how communities wholly enjoy the rituals and practices of creation of single components; the use of substances that broaden consciousness, and which extend perception, is a sort of collective experience. There is a very strong idea of group in this type of culture, and there is a great consideration granted to oneself and the other as components of a territorial and existential equilibrium. We have slightly forgotten this type of relationship, but, toward the end of the millennium, humanity needs to take account of these possibilities for freedom. Freedom always passes through knowledge of oneself, a deep knowledge. But this is still far from large numbers of people.

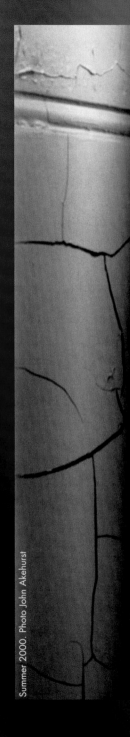

Summer 2000. Photo John Akehurst

What are the things that Costume National has changed in fashion?
The approach to dress; before the designs of Costume National dress was considered a "status," or in any case a form of costume tied to luxury, to an image that came out of the times of nobility, of the powerful class, of costumes that are lost in the nights of time; or else dress was the great revolution of the 1980s, which also included those fashion designers who decon-

Summer 1998

structed costume, a conception of fashion based on the desire to appear different from what came before, from a tradition, from the norms, and the distancing from a European concept of elegance in a radical and violent manner, using exasperated forms, immense shoulders . . . in any case a revolution of silhouettes with respect to what came before, with a totally different and at times anti-esthetic vision. I believe that Costume National detached itself a bit from all that and sought out an approach more closely bound to the individual, negating status and protest; but also thinking of that which we'd like to have to use it, to enjoy it, with a desire to modify the concept of status, no longer luxury, nor that of the noble who looks down over the street. A dress that you see, you like, that makes you feel good, a little like an anti-depressant! I've always lived fashion in this way, with the desire to feel at ease . . . That's more or less what Costume National has aimed for—the possibility of an individual choice outside of the constrictions of an "obligatory" fashion.

What type of methodology do you use when you design?
I work on a single piece, not on a total image, nor on a look; I work on single pieces that give the possibility of individually choosing a vision of the whole. I work on every single piece as though it were the only piece, not the whole, not the image that makes up that icon. Everything is born of a vision, of a concept that one then exemplifies in a technical act.

What is the alchemy by which a piece that you like, everyone likes?
I believe that anyone who creates anything has a sort of sensation . . . a moment in which they intuit whether something will please people or not. It's a sensation that is difficult to describe, a little magic, but there is a moment in which you know it . . . I can't tell you how or why, but you know

that thing will be liked more than the other, that is missing something . . .
Strangely enough, these alchemies work.
Do you also know when something won't be liked?
Yes, and sometimes you do it anyway, it could be a necessity . . .
Is it possible, as a threshold, that someone who does your same work might design bodies instead of clothes?

Summer 1998

I think so, I think that the future will hold for us some surprises that are more science fiction than we can think of, and that we'll experience them in an absolute normality because we'll be accustomed to them. At the moment my moral, my vision, my logic, and my desires make me think of this threshold with anguish . . . But all that, perhaps, when it happens, will already have entered into mentalities as "normal"; sometimes I think with infinite unease of how what just a little while ago was unimaginable is now completely normal for everyone . . . I don't know, the thinking structures of people, the architectures of thought will totally change, and maybe that won't be a mistake. . .
Predictions for the beginning of the millennium . . .
I believe that we must not forget about people, as we unfortunately did in the last century: people weren't the reason of this last century. The reason of this century was violence: the violence of a spent architecture, a senseless consumerism, an arrogant production. I maintain that when we forget people we pay a terrifying set of consequences, and so I hope that this type of mentality has a rapid ending. Human evolution has been possible mostly through emotions, sensations, and the capacity for imagination: shamans, artists, poets, the emotions of love, and sentimental privileges don't produce victims, but marvelous visions of the social interests at the center of the world.

Helen Storey

Photo Alan Reevell

Fabrics cut using ultrasound, glass fibers, polymers, composite materials—art and science meet in the world of fashion, in a conversation with one of London's most original creators.

interview by OLIVIA CORIO

Olivia Corio: Helen, you began your career as a fashion designer and then dedicated your energies to Primitive Streak, *a non-commercial collection exposed in art galleries instead of being shown on the catwalk. When is it that you went from commercial fashion to "artistic" fashion?*

Helen Storey: For ten years I managed a fashion house just like any other, which allowed me to do a little experimentation . . . but those were times in England in which the entrepreneurial world didn't help young fashion designers, and institutions didn't know or understand how to. It was very difficult to live in that situation. So I rapidly moved over to exportation, shifting eighty percent of my earnings to Japan and America; this made it possible for me to get through the recession that struck Great Britain in the beginning of the 1990s. Then I began to take into consideration the idea of making an experimental collection, something different . . .

Is Primitive Streak *your first collection to exile itself from the fashion world in the commercial sense of the term?*

It was an anomalous project, it wasn't conceived for being realized and set into production. Its goal wasn't to sell clothes, but rather to explain some of the processes that are very difficult for common people to understand.

You chose to use clothing to represent biological substances, such as an embryo in the first stages of development. In your collection there are actually some fundamental phases of embryo development represented, like fertilization and the formation of the nervous system and heart. This signals a radical break from tradition because biological processes have never been represented in fashion . . . Do you believe in a possible correlation or interaction between fashion and science in artistic terms?

I think that the scientific world is immense; it's a greater source of inspiration with respect to history because it gives importance to the way in which we came into this world, not how we lived. There are some fashion designers who have dealt excellently with history, like Galliano and Westwood, but I'm much more interested in the scientific world as a source of creativity.

What do you have to say about Primitive Streak, *what would you like to communicate?*

I worked with my sister, who is a biologist, who concentrated on the first thousand hours of a human being's life, with all that entails. She began by observing the cells; why they divide in the way the do, why they grow in a certain direction and not another, and cell differentiation. Then we needed to find a way to take those thousand hours and subdivide them into more well-defined parts . . . and I tried not to explain the more complex part of the process, something too difficult even for me to learn, but rather tried to fill a few of the gaps in the common people's knowledge. People know a bit about an egg's fertilization and have heard talk of DNA and similar things, probably from *Jurassic Park*, and they are familiar with the final phase of embryonic development; but there are really very few who know about the passages from one phase to the next . . . and so my work consisted of providing the missing information, from which I got the title *Primitive Streak*, which is the first, essential phase of an embryo's development. I didn't have a studio or a company backing me, I collaborated with the London College of Fashion. I only had three or four months to finish the work, a deadline that was decided upon by the Welcome Trust, who had invested in the project.

Your project was also realized thanks to the use of cutting-edge technologies: a fabric created with an ultrasound machine and a scanner, shoes with hydrolytic heels, fiber optics for electrifying the dresses, and a fabric created with the structure of DNA . . . What is the relationship between fashion and technology?

I think that fashion designers are obligated more and more to focus on technology. And it's necessary that they do so, because you can't go very far looking just at history without also focusing on substance. I think the future of fashion lies in textiles, because in

Primitive Streak. Photo Jason Lowe

trying to understand fabrics one also comes to understand the human body—it's almost a return to cellular content, a step far beyond what is visible to the superficial glance, going back to where things really began and start to experiment behind the scenes, and not on things already done. There is a lot of talk about intelligent fabrics, fabrics that know how to think . . . I'm not all that convinced, in the end; during some of the last seasons in which I was working commercially I had begun to use lavender flowers and roses because I wanted my dresses to create an atmosphere with their perfume. Back then we joked about it, but now I think that I'd put it into the yarns, in such a way that the fabrics themselves have their own perfume, a very precise scent. There is a lot of work to be done with technology and fabrics, but we still need to find a way in which fashion designers can apply technology in the commercial realm. It's a question of experimental textiles; one wonders how to make them last and whether they might create problems on a global commercial level; so the world of fashion is divided between those who want to experiment, making their mark on history, and those who don't. Fashion is moving too rapidly, and for all the wrong reasons. People rush just to make the commercial machine go round. It's that sort of velocity that has bothered me.

Primitive Streak. Courtesy of ICA, London

134

Manuel Vason

A very young photographer, and protagonist of the London scene, Manuel Vason transfers the energy he finds in art to the fields of fashion. Fascinated by the most advanced practices of contemporary art, he creates images that seduce through the beauty of tension at its extreme limit—decidedly sophisticated.

interview by FRANKO B

Franko B: Do you want to introduce yourself and talk a little bit about your background?
Manuel Vason: I began photographing five years ago, when I moved to Milan to work as an assistant in a large photographic studio, and I got closer to this world through fashion photography. I worked with the best fashion photographers (or with who was considered such), who taught me how to obtain quality lighting, or how to present myself with respect to the model, and also the mentality of group work. After a little while Milan began to seem very commercial to me, I felt frustrated and decided to leave; I thought London would be the ideal. I arrived in London a year and a half ago and found a job in a photographic studio. The work was the same as what I was doing in Milan, but I was maturing. Fashion photography is very limited, and too often they tell you what to do, so I focused all my energies on my personal projects, which weren't commissioned by anyone.
Talk to me about your projects and your influences . . .
I always work with fantastic people. What I learned working with the best fashion photographers is that they dedicate a lot of time to research, and believe in group work and collaboration. I got in contact with you because I'm interested in your performances and was thinking about the possibility of collaboration. Working together with you gave me new ideas and more energy for the next project.
The thing I most appreciate about your work is the passion of your photographs; I think this is what makes people special.
I believe in passion. I believe in the excitement that I feel when I push the shutter release button. I adore freeing my imagination and emotions and then playing with the person I have in front of the lens up to the point where the tension becomes something special. I wouldn't be able to do it without passion.
When you snap a subject's photograph, do you think of portraying it as it is or do you think that photography can change a person, that you're creating a mutation?
It's a mutation . . . my point of view and my imagination are what solidify on the photographic paper what I created in my mind. Sometimes I like to be realistic, but what can be realistic for me may not be at all realistic for someone else. There's always a process of transformation at work. Recently I

ventured out on a limb with different light sources in relation to simple nude bodies, creating an effect that was anything but realistic.

And now what is your dream?

I'd like to be assigned some jobs that leave me the freedom to take photographs as I like. For the time being I work just for myself, for my pleasure, for passion. I'd like to have the same energy twenty years from now.

Is there a fashion photographer that you admire?

I like how a lot of them work. One of the things that inspired me to become a photographer is a book by Richard Avedon, *Evidence*. I admire the way

he succeeded in articulating his personal documentary project of capturing the common people on the streets of America with his extraordinary worldwide campaign for Versace. That's definitely a success!

Becoming financially independent is the dream of every artist in order to be free to choose his own creativity . . . Can you tell me about how you work?

The biggest difficulty I've found since I started dedicating myself to photography has been finding my own personal style, a style that's all mine. I think that it's very useful to always use the same camera—a complicated, slow, imposing one (10" x 8"). The quality of the slides is incredible, but the cost of the film is invariably high. That makes the game even more exciting, because all the work lies in preparing the shot—one shot. And then I always try to use the same group of people and keep the lighting very simple.

DIESEL

an encounter with
RENZO ROSSO and MAURIZIO MARCHIORI
by FAM

FAM: Calvino wrote, "If I were to choose a symbol for welcoming the arrival of the new millennium I'd choose the secret of lightness." It seems that this symbol is also a little bit the philosophy of Diesel.
Renzo Rosso and Maurizio Marchiori: At just a stone's throw from 2000 Diesel put into action a project of change. You don't make the first operation of change on the market, but in your head, and that's important. The integration of old and new methodologies is the lifesaver for a company like Diesel, which wanted to spontaneously enact changes before they were even necessary. During such a period the company counts on the winning years, the years that allowed us to arrive at what Diesel is today: the choice of a culture and a mentality that since the beginning have identified it and made it recognizable without overwhelming its success valves. Diesel thinks of a new project, a design as a prototype for a new person, a new body, and a new face that is ready to face future challenges.

Situations, colors, faces, and a way of communicating the awareness of a lifestyle—an encounter with the protagonists of a philosophy that made lightness a mentality.

We had the great luck of living during the millennial transition and this is a unique experience, which Diesel sees as an epochal transformation. Even though we're considered "right," "ahead of things," "cool," and "transgressive," nonetheless we began to question ourselves, expressing a desire to change, a Diesel that "prepares itself" to express all its full potential. It's very difficult to "voluntarily" fall into a crisis, and this is our challenge, to be ready to modify ourselves, change according to the new demands and new subjects. A crisis is synonymous for change, and change is life.
What did Diesel want to be in the past, and what does it want to be in the future?
We began with a design that above all created a way of working together. Renzo wanted to form a working group with people united by the same life philosophy, a team that would have the same project, which wanted to work together having fun. No one was asked to modify his own way of being, but everyone was asked to maintain his own individuality. This was a winning mentality, because in the multiplicity of intents and perspectives that idea of Diesel grew; and we never thought to be capable of suffocating each individuality in the uniformity of the "group." Diesel strives to understand what happens within transformations and investigates, suggests, and invents garments that respond to both formal and behavioral

37°C
98°F

F/W 1997–1998. Photo Rankin

needs. In the future Diesel aims to define and develop the possibility of communicating one's own subjectivity through garments, objects, clothes that before all else transmit emotions and sensations . . .

Diesel has been the symbol of a slow engine . . .

The name is linked to the period in which Diesel was born; 1978 in particular, as it was the year of gasoline, alternative energies, and problems related to the exhaustion of oil resources. Actually we were the antithesis of all that a diesel engine is, even if we like the idea of a warm-up time before departure, a moment of reflection and then . . . you're off!

Diesel also represented a new way of communicating, an "antidepressant" approach . . .

Diesel wanted to cross a road close to the borderline, very close . . . At times the difference between being inside and outside that line was subtle, but we've always opted for irony . . . the nuances of color are innumerable, and we like to play with nuance and gradations! Irony has always been like aspirin for us, one has to learn to laugh, in some situations it's indispensable, otherwise events will just crush you . . . With irony you also learn to establish priorities. It's important not to become brutalized, otherwise you fall into a vicious, heavy cycle, creating a hostile environment around you, and that certainly isn't at the base of the lifestyle of someone who chooses to communicate even through their way of dressing. We have never chosen the route of shock as an end in itself, we wanted to launch some input, we chose a liberating laugh . . . and above all we chose to communicate out own choices, our own way of living. We created a sort of synergy between the company and its communication, to the point where we no longer distinguish the two . . . All this has to do with coherence, and people felt a coherence in our communication, even through the choice of media, through the horizons we used to exist.

Ever since its beginning Diesel has thought of a product and an international communication.

Ever since 1978 the idea has been to create a collection that could satisfy the planet, as opposed to a territorial ethnicity. Right at the beginning, actually, we thought it would be possible that a single product could satisfy an entire market and consequently, when we began our communications, in 1988–89, we used just a single mode of communicating—exclusively in English. Diesel garments aren't a uniform, but the possibility of a system of combinations; this is what people understood, just as they understood the humor of our communication.

One hears a lot, actually, about your way of communicating, from publicity and ads to parties and the events you organize, a planetary vision and feeling . . .

Here at Diesel everyone was asked to bring to the table, aside from their capabilities, also their own experiences, a collective communication that would move through life and converge in the image and the product. This is why Diesel doesn't produce uniforms, and instead seeks to pass on a message of possibility, not impossibility. Diesel wanted an image of lightness for itself, and, as Calvino said, lightness carries a great weight and is one of the elements of the near future . . . A sort of call to begin learning how to live and not just get by. This was the line that allowed us to arrive to today and which should permit us to continue. It's our desire to be "inside" events, and not just journalistically report them. It the 1970s it was necessary to be outside all frameworks; going against the current was a synonym for change. In those years it was necessary to break away; today the problem is completely different, today the problem is to come in through the right door, and we're still convinced—and this makes all the difference—that there is always a right door. Perhaps this is why our message always wins. We're here today, and in this time we want to be on the inside, acting here, now.

S/S 1999. Photo Rankin

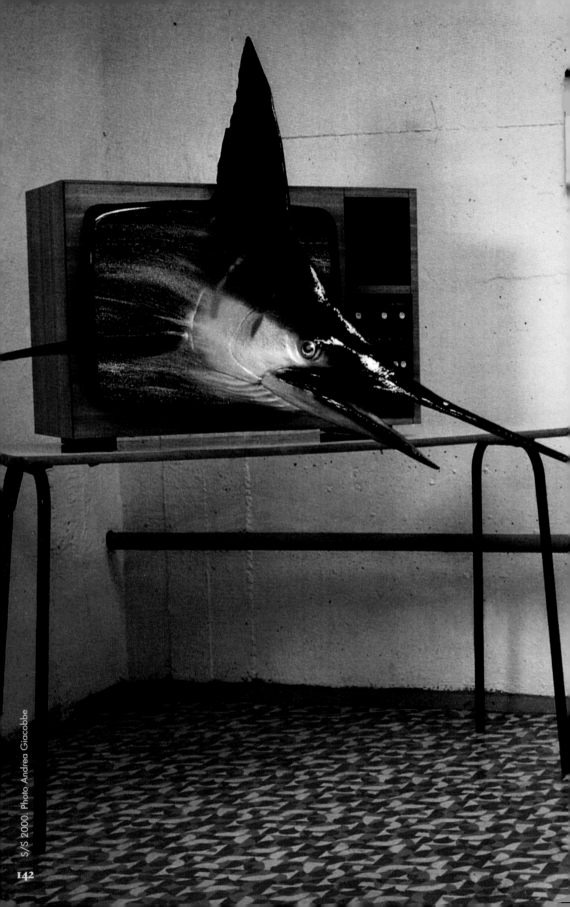

S/S 2000. Photo Andrea Giacobbe

Another challenge overcome by Diesel was that of reaching a trans-target audience . . .

Beyond just targets and marketing, we divided our production into two parts: the traditional target and the modern target, and naturally the latter is determined neither by age nor by other identity factors. The first is comfortable clothing for those who want to live in a world where they act directly, with everything within reach, a world without too many questions and demands that are, all told, realistic enough. The modern target, on the other hand, has a limitless world of references, clothing for those who want to go, search, discover, in a world full of questions and curiosity. A world full of *whys*, and a spontaneity that has kept the youthful desire to know, investigate, and risk. It's the target of who has chosen a mental horizon made up of enthusiasms, a universe in which one is a perennial student, with always the same desire to change; and, above all, has kept since childhood the ability to "cry" for two seconds and then move on. The adult world, on the other hand, is often stressed because it constantly rummages and makes things heavier than they are; there's a need to return to giving things the right weight. And, as you see, it's not a matter of age, but of mental openness. Right now values and relationships are being questioned; we're interested in participating in these discussions, even with a clothing line. Nothing can

change if we don't start by changing ourselves, in everything we do—not just the large things, but above all in the ideas of all that in our days and in our lives constantly accompanies us. All told, our productions develop over many moments—scents, light, movement, actions, bodies, clothing—with the conviction that today more than ever we live in a migratory universe where the choice of place makes up part of everyone's imagery. We live daily in a visual and aural environment and believe that the flow of time dedicated to oneself is very important, an individual and collective time that responds to the mood of individuals in continual metamorphosis. Diesel designs suggest that the reality that appears identical every day can

suddenly surprise us at the street corner, in our own home, in a transitory place. The clothing of the end of the last millennium has decided to live together with the people and places that form a positive mentality, a mental costume that wants to become all consuming, that pulses with the heartbeat of emotions and desires.

But what is clothing for Diesel?

Our goal is to dress people to "undress" them! Today dressing is like walking around the streets naked, because you express your character, sensations, and invariably your choices through your clothing. Clothing is often considered an end in itself, but in reality it's what betrays a behavior, a sensibility, a choice. Clothing is the dignity of being able to represent and express your self. This is the Diesel projection, to discover certain values through a certain way of dressing—this is our soul. Of course, we naturally want to sell, that is also important; but in the ideal ranking it's in second place, money interests us only inasmuch as it allows us to create our designs. We have demands on our budget, our time, and the numbers, but at Diesel it's imperative that *we do what we like to do*. To understand it's enough to pay attention to what's happening on the street, one has to be in the world. The street is a mass of information, you have to turn on your satellite dish, and your reception is amplified by reading, going to the movies, listening to music, and living . . . You need to maintain your own personality while adapting it to the times—that's what we want to do.

I seem to understand that the idea of the future for Diesel is blue . . .

Certainly, and not just because blue is the color of jeans . . . but above all because there is a need of color.

S/S 2000. Photo Andrea Giacobbe

RANKIN

He is the creative director of *Dazed and Confused*, the manifesto of the London trend of uncensored and ironic creativity; but before all else a photographer—of fashion, faces, skin— he seeks out the body through the lens. Bodies in movement, clothes on fire, models suffocated in cellophane—death becomes fashion, a fashion that makes use of everything, absorbing reality and transforming it into glossy pages.

interview by OLIVIA CORIO

Rankin at work. Courtesy of *Dazed and Confused*

Rankin: I began taking photographs at the age of twenty-one. At the time I was studying bookkeeping and lived with seven artists. I knew I was good at taking photographs. Then I went to the London College of Printing and as soon as I finished my studies I started a new magazine, aimed at students.

The current world of photography is inflated, because of the cult of the image created by magazines. It's not easy to find one's own style, and succeed in defining the main structures and character of one's own works. In what way is your photography evolving? Substantially, how do you create your own style?

Fundamentally, when I photograph a person, I'm very aware of the fact that the person, whoever it is, is in a certain sense collaborating with me. It's necessary to establish a sort of collaboration. I need to feel that they want to collaborate with me. My behavior is one of respect toward who is collaborating with me. And therefore it's in every effect a human relationship that I create with the person I photograph . . . I don't believe there's just one way of taking photographs, but then I think that it's right to always photograph in the same way. I've been criticized, for example, because I work with a white backdrop. I think that everyone is free to do whatever he wants. If you want to use a white backdrop, there's no reason not to. But I don't want to have a monochord photographic style; I believe in the graphics of the image, I believe in the form, and there is a lot to try out in terms of form . . . I also think that photography is a highly personal act, but I am equally convinced of the fact that a photograph cannot mean anything for me if it doesn't have meaning for someone else.

Photography, then, for you, is based on a human relationship . . .

Yes. And people are my main source of inspiration, meeting people. Both women and men inspire me, but women in particular.

I think this preference for women is evident in your photographs. They're the incarnation of eroticism. How much importance does the erotic impulse have in your work?

Let's say I'm at the height of excitation when I photograph robust women. I like women a lot, women of every type; I love their bodies. I remember in a magazine quiz once there was a question asking what was most pleasing about women's bodies, and I replied the difference between one body and another. The photograph of Helena Christensen, for example . . . I was obsessed with her skin, and I asked her to bite her arm very hard; the mark her teeth left on her skin was extremely erotic. I don't find that a girl of "small" stature is necessarily pleasing; it takes much more than just a certain size to make a woman seductive. The body is something . . . unique.

Photography, above all when it has something to do with the fashion world, is always a critical process. There is a sort of tension created between the artist's desire to be creative and free and the dictates of commercial success. One would say that you've resolved the problem with the launch of your magazine.

When we started the magazine we had the firm intention of making it, since we didn't want to work for others. We really put everything into it. It takes personality and concentration. Perhaps the peculiarity of my vision is linked to the fact that I grew up in the Thatcher era, when it wasn't permissible to be unemployed. There were only two alternatives: either you were unemployed and led a totally shitty life, or you were ready to take risks. Every time I put myself out on the playing field I think that just maybe I'll make it. The difference between our magazine and others is that we try to have a direct contact with celebrities and art. We try to be correct. The magazine's title, *Dazed and Confused*, says it all: we really are dazed and confused. The dominant approach evident in our magazine is that we interview people and snap the photographs. There are those who consider *Dazed and Confused* just a trendy magazine and nothing more, but if you read it it's not just fashion and images . . . there is also content.

From a postmodern point of view music seems to represent perfectly the concept of contamination . . . Sometimes it evolves so quickly that other forms of art get inspiration from it. Does music inspire your work in one way or another?

Music is one of the most important things in my life. It influences the way I do things. What sets music apart is that it's so profound, it moves you, it takes your heart and soul. I don't think that photography has the weight that music does. In many respects it's as if you were elaborating upon people. In portraits there is a mediation that occurs between the photograph and the artist. My behavior with regard to portraits is very collaborative, so I express my complicity in such a way that others trust me. I wouldn't talk though of postmodernism, I don't like the term postmodern, I use irony but don't consider myself a post-modern artist.

In London, where you live, photography covers a crucial role in the development of the latest trends, especially with the most innovative fashion . . . is it important to know in what direction photography in general is moving, and what its trends are? You see it, for example, in the shows, there are always more exhibition spaces dedicated to photography . . .

I think that it's always important to go and see shows . . . I think it's nec-

Burn

essary to go and see the work on exhibit, hung on the wall. The work itself is important, the reproduction will never be like the original, and if you look at the work in its original size you can really see it, and feel the sensations it provokes . . .

You've also ventured into filmmaking. How are photography and cinema different?

I think that a film is like a book, and photography like a joke, a tale. I aspire to be a filmmaker, but I always try to attain a greater depth with photography. I want to tell stories. It's more difficult to tell stories with photography because it's made of fixed images detached from one another. This is just the beginning of my work . . . I still feel the need to experiment, search, move ahead, and evolve. Deep down, I've only just begun!

Goldie

Walter van Beirendonck

Walter van Beirendonck's productions are like fractals, and are an invitation to remain rapt before the kaleidoscope of change—KISS THE FUTURE! The Boymans-van Beuningen Museum has dedicated a major exhibition to his work.

interview by FAM and VIVIANA DI BLASI

Summer 1994. Photo Ronald Stoops

The Boymans-van Beuningen Museum in Rotterdam invited Walter van Beirendonck–W.&L.T. to create a large exhibition event for Fall 1998. "KISS THE FUTURE!" became a context that was very particular and exciting, meant to present an alternative point of view on fashion in the museum. Instead of opting for a retrospective of the designs of W.&L.T. created by Walter van Beirendonck, they decided to concentrate on the installation of the current collection, *BELIEVE*, for Fall–Winter 1998–1999, which was presented during men's fashion week in Paris the previous January 25.
The show, which included 150 models in an immense filmmaking studio, was articulated in a fluid evolution beginning with baby clothing and casual

children's clothes and progressed up to a more mature cosmopolitan style, finally culminating in a limited edition collection. As with all W.&L.T. collections, the fashion designer's work was solidified in a multifaceted, 360-degree clothing line. Giving a closer look at the collection one sees an ulterior dimension, made up of a creative assemblage of various details, both functional and esthetic, that enrich the clothes with a positive message.

The Boymans-van Beuningen Museum presented this show in the context of a series of collaborations between designers and architects. For this reason Walter chose to work with Marc Newson, the Australian designer he had collaborated with on the global "shop-in-shop" design project for

Believe

W.&L.T. As an accompaniment to the show, the *BELIEVE* catalogue, published by the Boymans-van Beuningen Museum, illustrated the creative process of the fashion designer, beginning with the ideas and basic concepts, following the entire progression of designs and projects, until arriving at the definitive collection, presented as a fashion show on the catwalk. Walter van Beirendonck was the catalogue's art director, while the layout was done by Paul Boudens.

In the creative genesis of the W.&L.T. Fall–Winter collection 1998–1999, a single and fundamental cue led to the basic concept for the general make-up of the event. This cue, which later evolved into the "Reconstruct-Your-Face Makeup," took inspiration from the work of Orlan, the famous French artist who, through reiterated plastic surgeries, manipulates her own body and identity. Orlan's work is a point of departure for the research done by Walter van Beirendonck on the standards of beauty for the next millennium. For the fashion show he designed artificial protuberances, which were then created and applied to the model's faces by the prosthetic makeup artist Geoff Portass; Jürgen Teller did an exclusive photographic documentation of the event.

Virus Mutations: Is there an artist, either contemporary or from the past, with whom you share a particular sensation or sense of purpose?

Walter van Beirendonck: I am fascinated by art in general, and for some time have been attracted by artists like the Americans Paul McCarthy and Mike Kelley and their fantastic works. Recently I saw the show by Mariko Mori in London, and really liked it. Freedom and expressivity in art are important examples for me; after all, I am much more interested in what is happening in the art world than what is being done in the fashion world.

Summer 1989_Photo Ronald Stoops; illustration Jan Bosschaert

What does the body represent for you?

The body is our "base," which we use to express what we have inside. I think that EVERYONE needs to be proud of his own body, and the traditional concepts of beauty, or the so-called perfect measurements, have absolutely no value for me.

Do you feel as though you belong to a specific village or human group?
I am an individualist, and have no interest in belonging to certain groups. It's clear that I feel more in harmony with certain groups and less with others, but nevertheless I like to toss out the standards, subvert the rules, and provoke.

What does dress represent for you?
Stuff to wear, but above all that instrument I have chosen to express what I have to say as a creative person.

Is there a fashion designer, a practice, or a tradition that has inspired you?
I get inspiration from a lot of things, but certainly NOT from other fashion designers. In any case I respect and admire some of them, for example Comme des Garçons, Dirk van Saene, Martin Margiela . . .

What type of influence or effect emanates from the clothes and reveals the person wearing them?
Clothes can be important for expressing personal feelings, but I don't think that always has to be the case. Unfortunately, recently clothing is used more and more often to testify the stupid belonging to a group.

How do you interpret the fact that some groups circle around accords or reciprocal rules?
In reality I don't like that very much, because it proves the need individuals have to find confirmation in the behavior or rules of a group. But on the other hand it can be interesting and fun as a social phenomenon—something that creates fashion.

What do you think of plastic surgery and biological engineering?
All the recent experiments of cloning and biological engineering fascinate and scare me at the same time. I am sure that the life and fashion of the future will be directly influenced by the progress of this experimentation. Plastic surgery is one of the factors that have most inspired my latest collections. If it is used in a creative way it can be interesting for the beauty of the future; on the other hand, it becomes stupid and boring if used only to modify one's connotations. Creative bodily manipulation and the work of Orlan provided the inspiration for the makeup of *BELIEVE: PROSTHETICS AS ESTHETICS OF BEAUTY.*

Do you think it's possible that in the near future fashion designers will set themselves to designing bodies instead of clothes?
Already now, when I work on the look for an exhibition event I try to create an appropriate environment on the person who wears my outfits. The entire Avatar movement, as well, which exists in cyberspace, is greatly interested in the "creation of people" with absolutely no ties to traditional bodies. The clothes in the future of fashion will be more a limitation than a solution for creativity.

What type of person do you think of when you design an outfit?
No one in particular; I am extremely open and flexible as to who wears the clothing. For the fashion shows, instead, I carefully choose the models.

Earlier you said that the art world interests you more than the fashion world. What are the concrete elements in which a contamination between the two worlds is evident?
What I love about the art world is that the value of works constantly grows with the passing of each year; what I hate about the fashion world is that every six months you are judged based on a new collection. The old ones are good for the trashcan. It's so stupid.

Orlan. From *Believe* catalogue

Believe

Believe

The look of Alan Hranitelj knows no bounds. It's impossible to call them simply clothes, and they often approach "mobile sculptures" that, worn by sexless beings, recall a dream world in a gravity-free dance.

Photo Miha Skerlep

Alan Hranitelj

interview by VIVIANA DI BLASI

Psiha. Photo Miha Skerlep; direction Vito Taufer

Viviana Di Blasi: History, myth, fables, tales . . . your work is intertwined with the figures of a singular, superhuman typology. What is your human reference?

Alan Hranitelj: There is no explicit reference for my work. When I create I am aware of working with my intuition, with references that are the product of my spontaneous actions. I cannot, and do not wish to, predetermine and predict my creations, I simply sit down to work with a particular material that I have chosen; this interaction of the material with my hands and my mind assumes a particular form, it becomes the organism of an independent artifice, and is the result of a specific dialogue between two subjects: my person and the material with which I create. I don't have, and don't wish to have, a specific conceptual approach to my creations, a philosophical point of view that I would end up finding outside of myself. The only philosophy that exists is the here-and-now, in which I live and work in a state of spontaneity. History, myth, and fable are typologies against which I instantly rebel, in an aware or unaware way, using fragments of my memories of objects, images, and stories. Flowers, fruits, and stars are a part of my personal universe, and are objects with which I create my artifacts, my stories; but these can be substituted with other objects, depending on the creation of the moment and its needs. My "works" do not exist in time, and I never refer to a specific period or style; the style that interests me is my own personal one, which hasn't changed over the course of the years, from my first creations up to today. I am not interested in creating artifacts that can cause strong reactions within the public, or that please the public of the particular moment in which they are presented.

155

They need to live their stories and their personal histories, which clearly refer to the past and present but are not conditioned by those.

The world of fairies and witches is a single form. These two are no longer separable as in the obvious dualism of our social rules. What meaning does multi-identity have for you?
When I create theatrical costumes, like for the opera, for example, I work in a group; I proceed, then, in close contact with the directors and take action on the entire evolution of the theatrical work or opera. But, paradoxically, I do not forget my personal position as an artist, because I am naturally one of the creators of the opera. The interaction with the directors and other collaborators on determined parts of the work depends on the way in which the work in creation is defined step-by-step by the single personalities or approach of the individuals I work with.

A quick composite look at the Western pictorial tradition and fiction characterizes your outfits. What attracts you to the images you look at?
The attraction to the images and pictorial tradition does not depend on esthetics, beauty, or the novelty of the objects I look at. They can be horrendous, but they must attract me with something they have within, fragments of history, the energy they possess, and above all that *je ne sais quoi* that goes unnoticed and is not obvious to most observers. Sometimes it is a matter of the smallest details of the selfsame image, if not something actually indefinable. It is as if tradition and pretence were to float through the space surrounding me, enter into my mind, and continue on their way, while I carry on in my own way in my head.

Pierre et Gilles, David LaChapelle, excess, kitsch, irony, and a vision of existence that is absolutely outside reality; what are your interests?
I like the work of Pierre et Gilles just as I like a lot of other things, like Madonna or Peter Greenaway. I feel attracted to different art forms (and not just art): cinema, music, literature, and opera, but they are no more than just a part of life in all its components.

Body painting and fabrics, and cloth like baroque skin—what sort of life do you imagine for your artworks?
There are various types of elements in my creations. They can exist in theater or in reality, but in my imagination they are ready to live in a world that does not belong to this earth or to this age. Nevertheless they can exist, and they really do so in everyday life in a context that is the complete opposite of what one would expect.

Melanholija. Photo Romano Grozic

Tretje oko. Photo Romano Grozic

Butterendfly. Photo Miha Skerlep, direction Matjaz Pograjc

Armor-plating that re-designs the body's anatomies and voids its precariousness and fragility, mono-grams as modern brands, and cover-ings that blind with flashes of light and in-timidate the adver-sary; all these give a meaningful face to the concept of defense in one of the most meta-morphic elements of clothing of all times.

Bodies

RAMA

Alexander McQueen, F/W 2000–2001

Decorative hubcap of a parade wheel, with a Caravaggesque Medusa head. Milan, circa 1570–1580. Florence, Museo Nazionale del Bargello. Photo © Dario Lanzardo, 198

of Impact

TURE

by FRANCESCA CARAFFINI

Armature exercises a warrior-like attraction on the contemporary taste for the body that, even though it no longer needs to, chooses to cover itself in layers that structure, model, and cage it. These revisit not only medieval surcoats, but also the conception of clothing, which for centuries has only been the superficial covering of bustiers and rigid petticoats. And if the armature of the past carried, and still brings back to us, the names of its owners and their gestures, today it is the incarnation of the brand chosen by those who wear it.
Chain mail surcoats, precious metals, and forged iron have morphed into the ultra-resistant technological materials that are at the same time the flexible and light materials of urban daily life and strong new clothing.

Corselet, Innsbruck, Ambras Castle. Photo © Dario Lanzardo, 1987

Giger, *Watchguardian, head IV*, 1993

Jan Fabre, *Krijgers's Rosenkrans*, 1996

161

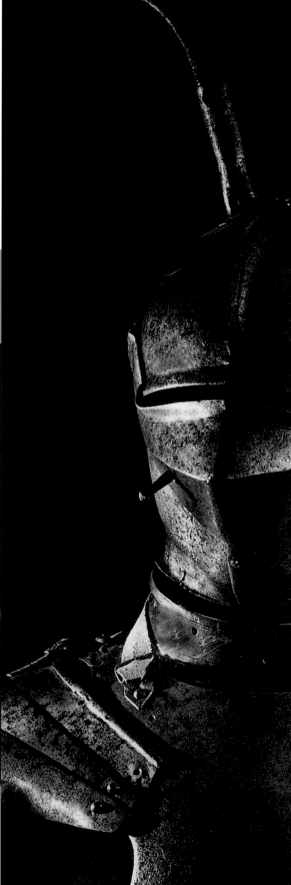

It seemed to you that the era of armature as knight's covering had ended? It's simply treading territory that is no longer a battlefield. Bikers covered in Kevlar and carbon fibers travel in urban agglomerates and modern gladiators challenge one another on the fields of existence, while the tutors of order are transforming themselves into truly "special" bodies, wearing

Jean-Paul Gaultier, F/W 1995–1996

armors that are no longer solely for defense but that also gather together within themselves the means for offense. But the true attraction that comes from this type of bodily covering derives from the inability to recognize who wears it; a "secret" that, up until the moment its identity is revealed, gives the body an impression of invincibility. And underneath the covering anyone could be hidden—even a woman; a motif that has inspired a majority of the epic literature now brought up-to-date in narrative film. From the innumerable versions of Joan of Arc to the futuristic sagas, the face is hidden, and the armor often hides a secret that cannot be confessed, like in *Star Wars*. A secret that remains protected, quite aptly, under the visor.

Warrior's armor known as "del diavolo" [of the devil]. Milan, circa 1485-1490. Udine, Sanctuary of the Blessed Virgin of the Graces. Photo © Dario Lanzardo, 1987

Ridley Scott's *Gladiator*.

Luc Besson's *Jeanne d'Arc*

Twenty random arma-turesque responses to cel-lular phone rings on the theme of armature 2001

by PAOLO BOCCHI

. . . volleyball player, armadillo, shrimp, rhinoceros, gladiator, crusader, tortoise, football player, ruff, boxer, biker, diver, kendo master, crocodile, Joan of Arc, lob-ster, armor-plating, scorpion, knight . . .

Northern Italy, mid-seventeenth century. Turin, Royal Armory. Photo © Dario Lanzardo, 1987

Alexander McQueen, F/W 1999–2000

Jousting corselet of Archduke Sigmund. Innsbruck, circa 1485. Innsbruck, Ambras Castle. Photo © Dario Lanzardo, 1987

Christian Dior Haute Couture. Photo Ruven Afanador

Housk Randall, Steve

Armature

1. a complex of defensive arms that ancient warriors wore

2. a temporary structure in wood or iron that sustains a tunnel or building wall

3. a metallic bone-structure in reinforced concrete constructions

4. in an electrical condenser, each of the two conducting surfaces in contact with the dielectric between them

5. an interweaving of warp and weft yarns that form a fabric

167

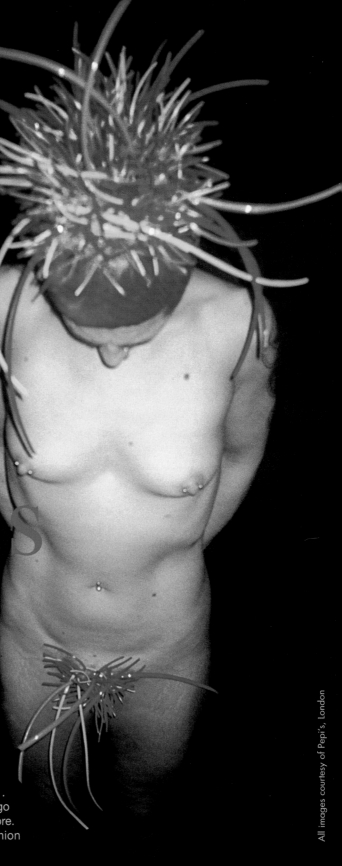

Carlos, Begoña, and Micky are the creators of Pepi's, a London coiffeur's salon of hairstylists who use prevalently recycled materials as extensions that modify hair into colorful, rigid masses.

interview by FRANKO B

Pepi's

Franko B: Carlos and Begoña have a salon where they are hairstylists and makeup artists, certainly in no banal way. Tell us about what you do.
Pepi's: I'm Carlos, one of the two partners at Pepi's (myself and Begoña). For ten years we had done hair and makeup, we were tired of doing something so commercial, and as hairstylists we were at the top; so, we decided to insert new materials into the hairstyles, things that had never been used before. We're totally different from any other hairstylists . . . we don't do it for money, and we try to go where no one has ever ventured before. We used to collaborate with fashion

designers, fashion shows, magazines, but we don't anymore because every one of them tells us that what we do isn't commercial. Sorry!

You've also exhibited at London's Torture Garden . . .

Yes, they asked us to show a little of what we can do. We worked with them on various things, fashion+hairstyling+makeup, and other things which have nothing to do with our work.

What are your clients like?

A bit of everything comes to us: kids, the youth, old people, everyone from bums to managers. I'd say we have clients of all social classes, who conduct different lives, but who are in any case people with a simple, very open mentality. We like normal people who always have the same face, we detest impostors and also gays; there was a time that we liked to work with them, but now they're all so concerned about non seeming male . . .

You work a lot with a Spanish group called Freaks; can you tell us briefly what sort of collaboration there is between you all?

The Freaks are friends with a background very similar to ours. We've known each other for a long time, and they're people like us who experiment with new images and new modes of self-expression.

What future does Pepi's have as a business?

Yes, we opened a salon in Tokyo in 1998, we chose Tokyo because the people want something different, they want to try out new things, and even more importantly, they have a profound sense of respect. In Japan it does not matter what look you have or how you think about things—they always treat you as a person. We've encountered endless problems in Europe and the United States, but not in Japan: aside from Tokyo, London is the only city where you can work without worrying too much about your image.

Here you are very extravagant originals, but in Japan there are a lot of people with an extravagant look. Do you find that interesting?

It's very interesting to be in a place where there are a lot of people like you, who don't judge you by appearances. We also like the fact that people dress well every day, all day, seven days a week. Not like in Europe, where people often dress well only for society life; they're not real, it's just a matter of pretentious people who are trying to put on airs. What's difficult is to be extravagant when you have to go to the doctor, the supermarket, in the bus, or the subway; it's easy to be extravagant in a club!

What do you think of an artist like Orlan, do you think there are resemblances?

We greatly admire both Orlan and you, we consider you pioneers in your work because you know how to use your body like a painter uses the canvas. In some respects we resemble one another, but our manipulation is—for the time being—less physical than yours, even if it's still a manipulation that digs down into fantasy and becomes reality. It's a way of comparing our interiority with what's on the outside.

Recycling . . . talk to me about it, because yours is a true philosophy, using recycled materials.

We recycle almost everything: the salon's interior design and furniture are all made of garbage. It's a philosophy that stems from our being against consumerism; we try to make organic decorations in which things change, evolve, and deform over time. We want the salon set-up to modify, and we also want to make access difficult, because tourists cause a lot of problems for us, they come into the salon and treat us like monkeys at the zoo. And we do all we can to keep them out.

Photo Baby Jane

Fausto Puglisi

A protagonist of the new generation of fashion designers, already in his first collection Fausto Puglisi enchanted with the glittering of bodies covered only in synthetic diamonds. At the age of only 22 he was chosen by some of the heroes of the star system, from Almodóvar to Rossy De Palma, and Cher to Marilyn Manson . . . and new "coverings" are in the works . . .

interview by FAM

Ru Paul for Fausto Puglisi: Photo Baby Jane

S/S 1999 . Photo Pedron

FAM: What, for you, is creativity?
Fausto Puglisi: Creating, for me, means primarily exasperating desire, passion, and carnality. I hate anyone who poses the problem of a woman going to the supermarket.

Do you think of one woman in particular when you design your dresses?
The woman I have in mind is a Hollywood goddess, and at the same time a very normal one. She knows she's beautiful and because of this, at the base of her existence, there's the necessity to be desired. Her life is a novel that she herself writes. She's a dreamer, but also maladjusted.

Sensual and bewitching, your dresses are forms of bait . . .
Well, I think that by now sexuality is an optional thing, I mean that the time has come when we can be free to be ourselves. I think that in the span of ten years lots of things will change. Woman will be the true warrior, while man will become a sexual object. It's a waste of time to talk about homosexuality rather than bisexuality. We've already entered the third millennium, in continual search of new mutations: arms covered in diamonds, six fingers, crystal fingernails, and steel teeth. Here, try to translate these images into a dress, make James Dean put it on, and the game is over.

You were born in Messina and live between Milan and New York . . .
I love New York immensely. It's my source of inspiration, a continuous creative laboratory. A work in progress straight out of Genesis . . . no other city resem-

bles it. The past is erased, and remains only in memory. People often don't think about it, but Manhattan is completely surrounded by water: I was born in Messina, and the sea was my first love. In New York everything is bigger, Milan is too bourgeois . . . I don't love the system, so everyone thinks I'm self-ish or spoiled or badly behaved. I am a Mediterranean par excellence, on the one hand strong roots, on the other a curious voyager like Marco Polo. Everything I do is a product of this innate calling to discover. I've always had in mind certain works by Antonello da Messina; my obsession is the *Madonna and Child* by Fra Ange-lico—gold, light, strength, and color. Then I try to imagine her at Grand Central Station in New York, among the steel of the trains coming and going . . . When I design a dress, I always think of instinctive desires, I detest a certain false intellectuali-ty in fashion. Speed: I was a waiter at the Tribeca Grill and in the same period was designing the jewelry dresses for the movie *Showgirls*. In America eve-ryone opened doors for me: Cher, Marilyn Man-son, Ru Paul. It's easy to communicate with these splendid agitprops.

How are your clothes born?

Before designing I start with the presupposition that a dress needs to mir-ror a sense of the future, or in any case contempo-raneity. What would Vel-ázquez's *Infanta* be with-out the rigid architecture of her dress? Fashion is always linked to the future needs of society, and because of that it must

S/S 1999. Photo Pedron

After only two
collections
Tristan Webber
has become one
of the leaders
of London's
new generation
of fashion
designers. He
studied fashion
design and
marketing at
Southeast Essex
College of Arts
and Technology,
and attended
St. Martin's
in London.

Tristan Webber

interview by MARCUS WOODCOCK

Tristan Webber: The collection is the unfolding of several different themes that I've dealt with in the past, like physiology and anatomy, and which I try to approach from time to time, in each collection, in a different way. This is called DANAIDES, a compound name made from two words: DANA is a dragonfly in the larval stage, halfway between the chrysalis and the moment in which it opens up, and NAIDES. DANA and NAIDES form DANAIDES. The NAIDES are marine creatures from Greek mythology, a sort of siren, but more human: a cross between woman and fish. And even in this case I gave the name to a species, to a variety of woman. But the opposite is also true, because if the Danaides call to mind organic and bio-logical creatures, in the collection I use metallic parts and elements, metal-lic structures designed in such a way that the dresses adapt to the bodies with the specific, almost surgical, function of supporting. At the root of everything is the current use of titanium fittings inside the body and the insertion of objects below the skin. It's a way of bridging the gap between the metallic components spread throughout the body, forming a canal that functions as a passageway through the skin. With the chrysalis, beyond its biological connotation, I was looking for a logical and mechanical bodily structure and the transition into biotechnological constructions. All of us are readapting our bodies with a series of implants: years of technology have made us androids, even if in an imperceptible, subtle way such that we didn't even notice. I've come to use some components within the body so that an organic part and a logical, mechanical scheme would be found together.

Marcus Woodcock: Is this an optimistic thing?

Yes, I think that what I do is very optimistic; I look ahead without simmering in gloomy, melancholic predictions about the future, while I observe the human being as it transforms itself into a soft android. I'm not a robotic mon-ster. I am interested in the ambiguities of our being subjected to a physical transformation, and I believe I'm observing it with a very positive attitude.

Does this change have to do with the practical aspect or with beauty?

In this phase it's practicality and beauty together. With time the practical aspect will gain greater importance as it develops. For the time being all that interests me is the conceptual fact and the physical aspect. But there are obviously practical applications, in clothes that can be worn. As the collection evolves I have clearer ideas about the commercial aspect of it, and I know I want to deal with accessible clothes as well. But I need to sat-isfy my interior impulses that drive me to this sort of things as well.

Why did you decide to make clothes?

I began early, at eleven, twelve years of age I already wanted to make clothes, I was interested in the exterior aspect of people and clothes, I was fascinated by the manipulation of the image and superficial aspects of the human body: so I began to collect advertising images. They fascinated me, what was portrayed in them seemed so saturated with artificiality; people found them pleasant, whereas I looked at them with irony even if obvious-ly, given my age, I wasn't yet able to speak of it in these terms. It's from there that my interest came about, and has continued to grow.

Did you find the things that garnered general approval ironic?

Yes, it was extremely artificial, also because at the time it wasn't techni-cally possible to digitally manipulate or construct the images; everything was portrayed in a much cruder way with the technologies of the time, and you knew quite well that those images really didn't represent the person

177

that was photographed. They were false images of unreachable people, and the fact that they were used to sell products—makeup, dresses, lifestyles, attraction—I liked immensely.

Are you aiming at something in particular?
Are you trying to understand what point of view I'm starting from and in what direction I'm going? There aren't any; I'm working, I have various interests. The thing that most irritates me is when journalists have a look at the collection and sum up what they think in two sentences, whether it's a way of dressing with a strong sexual imprint or the lack of attention to quality, the quality of the design. Lots of them underline the fact that this collection is so sensational that it passes a vulgar judgment on color; but I just don't understand it, because these clothes don't fall into the mental categories they've made from looking at other fashion designers. They spend too much time criticizing people with their stupid worthless job; it can also be fine, I'm open to criticism, but what always jumps out is that they appreciate something a fashion designer does for six or seven seasons in a row.

You create clothes, but to draw attention to your clothes it's necessary to draw attention to yourself and your persona. So what do you think, then, of celebrity?
Celebrity is irrelevant, I think it's a stupid thing, you know what I'm trying to say? The fact that your name has circled the world and that people talk about you all the time everywhere doesn't change the fact that you don't have a cent and so it's very difficult for you to do things. Too much attention is given to celebrity. I don't want to be a celebrity. It's all artificial . . . It's like in interviews: my opinion changes from one journalist to the other. That's part of the game, right?

Kei Kagami

interview by OLIVIA CORIO

After studying architecture Kei Kagami found the most immediate form of expression for his creativity in fashion. Following collaborations with John Galliano and Issey Miyake he focused on a collection bearing his own name, a collection that is the result of a profound internal search, where clothing becomes a complex structure around the human body.

Olivia Corio: You began your design career as an architect. Why did you then move on to fashion?

Kei Kagami: I would say that, looking back, it makes no difference that I studied architecture and not fashion. I simply wanted to express myself. I needed a means of expression. I still like architecture but, as I already said, I simply wanted to express something that came from my mind or from my body. As far as fashion is concerned, I am able to think of a model, I am able to do it by myself, and I can wear it; I can do it all on my own. This means that I can express myself in every phase of the process. And on top of that I like to work with my hands, I think it's a magnificent thing. Regarding architecture, if I want to make a house, for example, I need money and hundreds of people to construct it. Making clothes is the most immediate way of communicating. If I want to express some feelings like anger or happiness it's enough to just sit down and draw.

Your clothing is often very structured. In a certain sense it seems inspired by architectonic forms. Is this true?

I don't deny that my clothes have something to do with architecture. It is clear that it inspires me, but not visually. Perhaps it is a very different approach. It is more . . . mental, and I would say more abstract. I let splendid buildings move me, I struggle to keep all that emotion within me, and I try to relive it when I design; I remember the intensity with which it impressed me on an intellectual level.

I find the idea of a space between body and dress very creative, a sort of dimension to find between the two. Is this also a result of architectural study?

After having studied architecture I thought of clothing as a sort of house, the house closest to the body, the nearest space; then came the furnishing, house and, finally, society. So the clothes we wear are the first shell of the human body. But there is still a space left between body and clothing, and it is there that you can create and, in a certain sense, invent.

The fact of wearing clothing like a sort of house is visible in forms like the tent-jacket, a normal sports jacket that can be transformed into a small tent. It mirrors the need to travel and adapt oneself quickly to the new environment. It's a new elaboration of the state of being nomadic, in the sense that an individual moves through different spaces . . . Now let's talk about materials. You have used accessories—like zippers—in a constructive way; that is, you have designed skirts and jackets made entirely of zippers. Is this a way for a functional element to become decorative?

No, I like functional beauty a lot, and I appreciate it. I love simple beauty—things that are simple but creative. I don't think that my clothing is only decorative. I always try to pair something simple and something creative; the pairing of simplicity with any other thing, from anger to beauty to every sort of feeling. But each time I want to add simplicity. For me clothing is not decoration, it is essentially the functional casing of the body. When I got the idea of a fabric made up of zippers, I thought of its possible functions; later, when I began to make the model, I discovered that I could make it constructive, and at that point I began to think of the esthetic structure that could be given to it.

Technology—how much importance does technology have for you? Does it influence your work, or your way of organizing the creative process?

Nowadays everything is becoming more technological, but I do not feel very involved. I think that everything must begin with a very personal and intimate impulse. The primordial idea is only in the brain, and only later you do need pen and paper. Perhaps technology influences my work, but the manner in which I conceive of the design is solely intellectual.

Dynamism is becoming one of the crucial elements of fashion. The idea of a person in motion, a dynamic life, is essential for the development of fashion and the trend toward comfort and sports clothing. In creating a collection do you give importance to the concept of movement, to a garment made for allowing the body to move freely? I ask because your clothes are so structured, almost couture . . .

In the 1990s there was a sort of naturalistic vision of fashion, which led to minimalism and to the idea that the clothes must not in any way constrict the body. The 1980s, on the other hand, were much more constructive; I grew up in the 1980s, and I was very influenced by design. I think that we are now arriving at the end of another decade and that moving forward perhaps a new concept of tailoring work will be born. As far as I am concerned, I absolutely want my clothes to be comfortable, and I always try to make portable things because I design clothes, I don't like to say that I am a fashion designer. In a certain sense I don't follow the trends, I like clothes and I like to make them myself, that's it.

What is your idea of beauty?

Each time I see beauty in something different. The idea of beauty changes along with me. In a certain sense beauty is my style of fashion. An idea, a story, an impression can all be magnificent. I always ask myself what I see beauty in: in society, in people. I think about what happens in society, and it is a very important moment for me. My life also influences my way of working, my mood, and my way of creating clothing.

Photo Steve Savege

Manuel Albarran

Manuel Albarran is the founder of Freaks, a group of self-defined fashion-performers. Manuel is a very complex designer who, through his own creations, deconstructs and modifies the human form. He is based in Barcelona, but is present at the most interesting manifestations of performance art and most important fetish clubs throughout Europe.

interview by FRANKO B

The world in which Manuel Albarran creates and designs is extremely complex. It's all a change of scenery, one feels unprepared, inexpert, with nerves ready to snap. Manuel has cultivated and developed his talent over the course of many years, working mainly in Barcelona. On his own and with the Freaks he's gained the unconditional support of Europe's best fetish clubs. The models and representations of Manuel Albarran shatter the chains of style, image, and acceptance. His design disassembles the human form. Feet become hooves, male becomes female, fetish becomes normality, all with a visually astounding final effect.

Franko B: Why "Freaks"?
Manuel Albarran: I think the name Freaks reflects the personality of my performances.
How many personalities do you have?
Sorry, I can't answer!
What influences you?
The world.
Barcelona . . .
I have my studio in Barcelona, where I prepare the collections and work on new designs. I am my own manager in my studio, and every day I work on new ideas.
Where do you exhibit, with whom, and in what sort of club?
I currently exhibit mostly outside of Spain, primarily in fetish clubs like the Torture Garden, where I held my last representation last December. In Spain mostly at private parties or at the Erotica Market more than anywhere else, but also at events that combine art and fashion. It wasn't easy for me in Spain, at the beginning I was an anomalous, scandalous person, and my performances weren't met with the welcome that I had hoped for; now it's not like that anymore. My collaborators, like Antonita Glamour To Kill, Mia, Miguel Guri, are mostly Spanish; but I also work with elements of other groups, like Citron and Rafit. They are people that understand my works and are open to accepting new ideas.
And how do the authorities react to you?

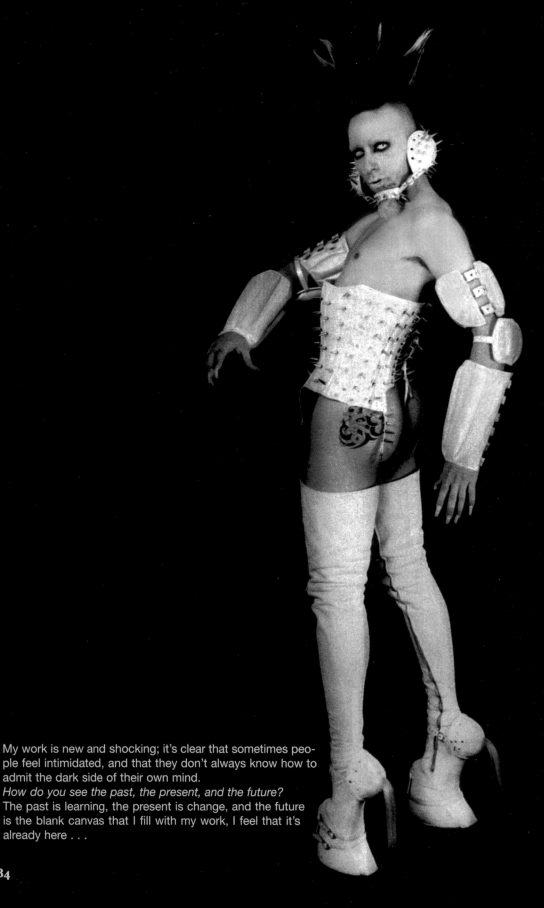

My work is new and shocking; it's clear that sometimes people feel intimidated, and that they don't always know how to
admit the dark side of their own mind.
How do you see the past, the present, and the future?
The past is learning, the present is change, and the future
is the blank canvas that I fill with my work, I feel that it's
already here . . .

An encounter with Carol Christian Poell, the 33-year-old Austrian fashion designer specialized in men's styles who in 2005 presented his first women's collection, which will doubtlessly be followed by a second and third . . . High-fashion styles and organic, experimental materials . . .

Carol Christian Poell

interview by LUCIANO CIRELLI

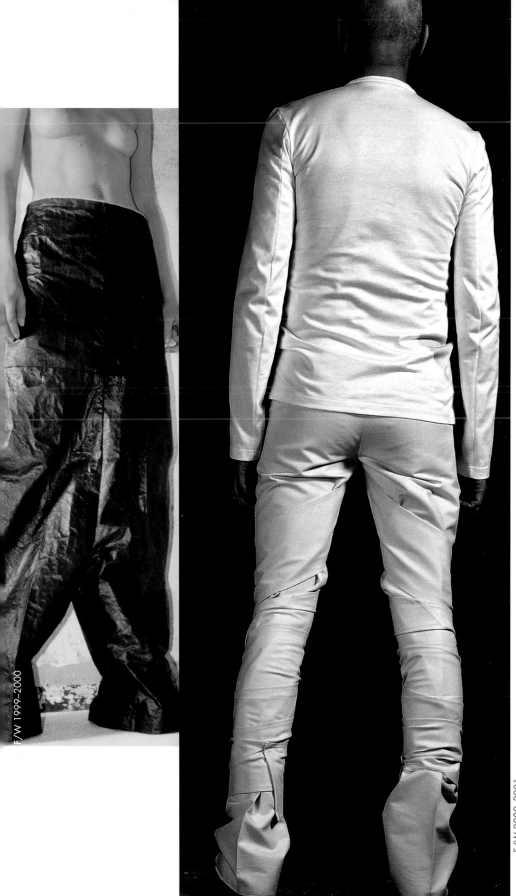

jacket, but there still is not everything, there will also be a shirt . . . in the trilogy there will be space for everything, but I want to do one thing at a time: "monotypology." I am very interested in focusing, concentrating my work on a single garment. Where is it written that I have to do a complete collection . . . I want to concentrate on a single garment to make it read well.

Do you think that in the second passage of this trilogy—the next collection in October—this message will be clearer?

I do not know, but I think not. Certainly it could be better clarified through the media, the press; it is more difficult to explain it to a customer because for him you can do whatever you want in a fashion show, on the condition that you have the pieces to put in the showroom.

Is it perhaps a condition more linked to the female body? Men need more complete clothing?

Yes, this was initially a project for men, but then it didn't seem so appropriate . . . it should have been the Sping–Summer 1999 collection, which was never realized. The men's collections in any case have had a total look since various seasons; it seemed correct to begin the women's collection with a new story.

Do you see differences between making clothing for men and for women?

Women's collections are very limiting, contrary to what I expected. With the men's collection I am able to push myself a lot without falling into the ridiculous, regardless of the two extremes of saying too much or not saying anything: there is a very subtle line where you can easily fall. With the women's collection I expected to be able to do anything, and instead I realized it is much more limiting because it is so normal to exceed, to fall into excess.

Perhaps the line you speak of is broader and so you grow accustomed to it, you are easily distracted . . .

On a woman anything goes well and so it is less stimulating, and more banal.

The body, be it male or female, is to be beautified or is it to be clothed?

To be beautified I wouldn't say, that serves no purpose. Even for me sometimes it is important to be aware of the uselessness of what I do. I begin with the presupposition that I must clothe, I clothe a person because in some way he needs to be covered (since the beginning). Clothing is a means of self-expression for people, it is an idiom; I give them some words!

F/W 1999–2000

192

John Willie

Here we publish some images from the late 1950s by John Willie, the photographer who collaborated on, among others, the American magazine *Bizarre*. The glamour and contemporary feel of these photographs is absolutely incredible.

by CRISTIANO DI GIOVANNI

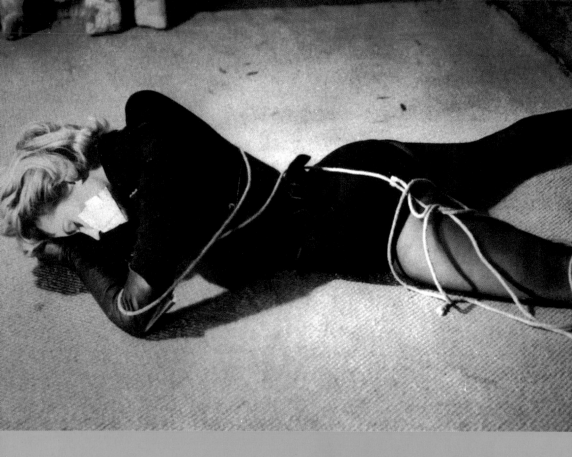

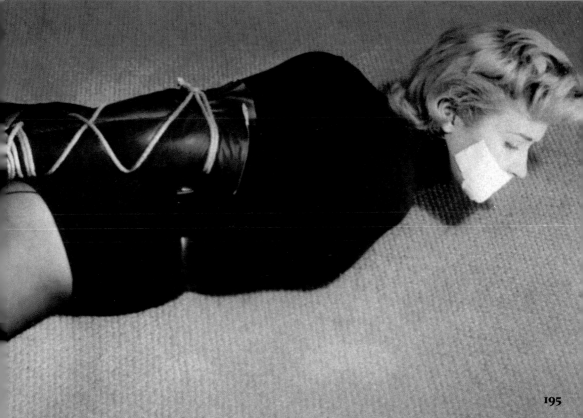

John Alexander Scott Coutts, in art John Willie, was born in Singapore, educated in England, lived in Australia and America, and died August 5, 1962, in Guernesey.

He "enchained" women, who were invariably beautiful, often all decked out, and certainly complicit. With a variety of effects: a face, an ornament, or a manner of submission. The esthetic ideal of John Willie lay in an inaccessible situation halfway between the "bondage" as the body and the model as an object. The circulation of desire establishes itself through a line that links the body of the binding to the body of the model, thus creating a third body composed of the first two—inseparable, as in a love affair of Cronenbergian recollection. From Pierre Molinier and his studio-laboratory, to Helmut Newton and his princely suites, one recognizes the attachment that numerous, inspired erotomaniacs have for impersonal but safe spaces. One recognizes also the modus operandi by which Jack the Ripper conducted his victims into his own home with the goal of perpetrating, in the most complete calm, his terrible crimes. Between artists and assassins there circulates a tradition of sweet violence with a domestic character. Undoubtedly John Coutts and Hans Bellmer must have, on occasion, had to prove their very hard will. Certainly Jack the Ripper had to be lovable and persuasive, like Landru on the road for Gambais. Regardless, whatever the nature of their crime was, all of them had but one motive: to go back home. À propos this fact, Pierre Molinier, closing his door, sealed on the doorknocker an unsurpassable final expression: *I've killed myself. The key is with the doorman.*

Gilbert Simon-Berger, *La Flotte-en-Ré,* March 1985

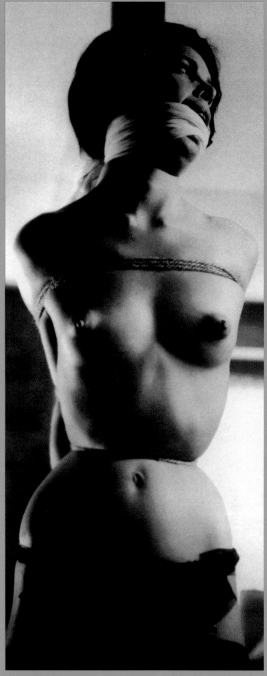

Alain Mikli

Photo J. B. Mondino

An encounter with Alain Mikli, Mr. Eyeglasses, the Architect of Sight, creator of the glasses favored by Jean Moreau, Bono, Wim Wenders, and Lou Reed, Philippe Starck's "accomplice" with the collection *Starck Eyes*, and inventor of the video camera-glasses. This year his marked talent for technology transforms him into a creator of re-combinable outfits

interview by FAM

Solaire, ref. 5671

Video camera-glasses, 1998

Panoramic sunglasses, which have a miniscule video camera positioned on the earpiece and were presented in Paris in 1997, have become a new instrument for seeing and "taking in" the surrounding reality. Naturally, they're by Alain Mikli, the man who transformed glasses into an indispensable fashion and technological accessory, a veritable esthetic prosthetic. In 1991 he created glasses for Wim Wender's film *Until the End of the World*, he made Uma Thurman's glasses in *Batman & Robin*, and he designed Jean Reno's face for *Godzilla*; he is the inventor of glasses without screws, and in 1996 together with Philippe Starck he signed the collection *Starck Eyes*, in which the traditional hinge is substituted by a biomechanical articulation conceived as a micro-clavicle inspired by the natural intelligence of the human arm. Currently, after video camera-glasses, he is entertaining his dream of constructing "humanitarian glasses" for the blind, a sort of information center connected to an urban station that guides, informs, and aids the movement of the blind—a project he is already working on.

FAM: How is the future for you?

Alain Mikli: It is a future in which technology can facilitate and amplify human possibilities. For some time already it has been possible, with a minor operation, to eliminate vision problems, so glasses, as we know them today, will become obsolete. I am designing and creating glasses with other functions: glasses that can film, photograph, send images via the Internet, and with Philippe Starck I am studying a model that, thanks to an internal wire, is capable of receiving and emitting sounds—telephone-glasses . . . It is a hybridization of the senses, between seeing, hearing, and so on, all the way to touching, tasting . . . It is a sensorial conception that perhaps, paradoxically, is more natural, a sort of activa-

Optique, ref. 2701

tion of the whole sensorial sphere able to receive and transmit stimuli. *This line of thought reminds me of Stelarc, the Australian artist who talks about the obsolescence of the human body . . .*

Barbie for Alain Mikli, 1999. Photo J.P. Metaye

It's not just a problem of obsolescence, but of an almost "natural" evolution of the species, toward a modified environment that requires individuals to have totally revolutionized sensorial and communicative capacities. I think of a being that can interact and intervene in the world it lives in with a real awareness and a series of new possibilities. I don't particularly love the "invisible" technologies; my video camera-glasses could have been made with smaller technologies, but I don't like the image of the "spy," it is not a question of "stealing" images, but rather the possibility to use data and information. The "natural" use of technology, on the other hand, I find very interesting—not fakery . . . Perhaps my concept of natural is a little particular, but I find that technology should be like clothing, equally visible and "portable," wearable; I think of convenient, comfortable, practical instruments, but not invisible and mimetic ones.

All the technologies of the end of the millennium were thought of as prosthetics that extend and modify human sensorial capabilities; is it the same for glasses?

Naturally, the video camera-glasses project moves in that direction, just as it is natural that our imagery is configuring itself in reality through the re-appropriation of techno-informational instruments that for many individuals seem to represent the realization of a collective intelligence, of a more intense participation in social acts and life. In all probability the new technologies will greatly modify our way of life, and within them we will be able to make several levels of existence coincide. With video camera-glasses, for example, we could discover new points of view still unknown in various

William Christie for Alain Mikli, 1984

Evelyne Bouix for Alain Mikli, 1989

Sapho for Alain Mikli, 1982

fields, such as sports or theater; artists or athletes could, by wearing this kind of glasses, give back to the public fully and in real time all their intensity and the same images and emotions that they are experiencing during a performance, a race, or a concert.

The characters in William Gibson's stories have glasses implanted directly on their skin and connected to their brain . . . are they Mikli glasses?

I think they must be! Jokes aside, I am very curious about and interested in forms of human-technological hybridization, inasmuch as they are used as a form of expansion of perceptive and cognitive possibilities. William Gibson's characters are for the most part using technologies that already exist, nothing too unreal or impossible; certainly, there is a little "exaggeration" in the instruments, but all told his future, and the future written by authors like him, is not such an improbable future. I think of the future as a form of contamination between all human cultures, and it will depend on each of us to act in such a way that this contamination does not rapidly become a leveling or homogenization. There are already signs of a form of "cultural epidemic"; look at McDonald's, an example of globalization but not of greater possibilities. Don't you think it's stupid to eat a hamburger in Milan? There, that is an example not of contamination (by the way, I find the name *Virus* superb for a magazine) but rather of substitution of habits and cultures. We need to preserve human dignity at all times, and this is true in general, for technologies and cultural couplings: there is nothing negative or positive on its own, and as always it is the use one makes of it that determines the sense of it all.

What type of relationship is created between eyes and glasses?

A sentimental one, naturally!

F/W 1999-2000

Materials like gold, porcelain, and Murano glass transform and mold themselves like prosthetics around the body that wears them. These are some of the elements used by Antonio Berardi, enfant terrible of the new scene of London couturiers. From his Sicilian roots Berardi takes the idea of a matriarchal society, with strong women, but in the dresses of baroque Madonnas.

Antonio

Simon Costin: In what ways do you prepare for a new collection?
Antonio Berardi: About a month before presenting a new collection I begin to think of the next one. The cue can be the idea for a dress that doesn't necessarily fit into the collection I'm working on at the moment, but could be an idea strong enough to be worth working on in a later line. I try also to think of new ways of beautifying things and new materials not often used in fashion: gold, glass, wicker, porcelain, and wood.
One might say that you nurture a true passion for some of the traditional, almost artisanal, methods—lace and embroidery, glass, etc. Where does this passion come from, and for what reason is it so important to you?
I grew up with my grandmother and an infinite number of aunts who were constantly embroidering and knitting. My mother and her sisters all prepared their own trousseau, because money, in 1950s Sicily, was scarce indeed; at that time the oldest daughter learned to become a seamstress and embroiderer from the nuns in the town convent. Keep in mind that in those years a lot of people emigrated, and people were willing to pay for something to take to America or wherever it was they were going, and those who had already left returned to visit their parents and wanted to buy

F/W 1999-2000

Photo Dan Lecca SP, 2000

Berardi

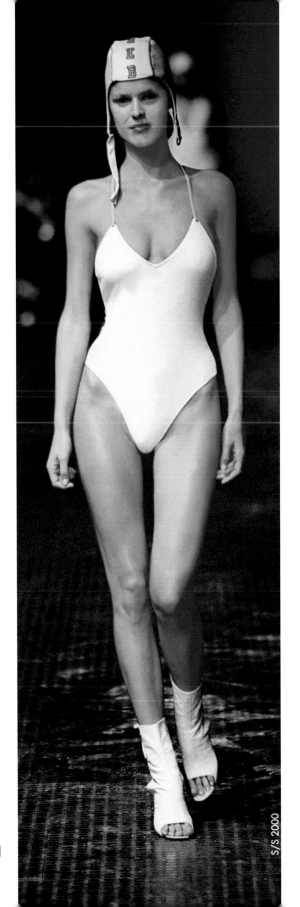

S/S 2000

interview by SIMON COSTIN

traditional objects to bring home or give as gifts: it was considered—and really still is to this day—a way to keep the memory of one's origins alive. One must also remember that patience is a virtue, and today there aren't many who embroider or crochet because it's a lot of work and the same things can be reproduced by machine. That's why I opted for embroidered lace; I knew it was probably the most demanding manual work of all, and in fact it was applied to the clothes only in tiny quantities. I began to want to use it more. It's also an English tradition as much as an Italian one, so unites both of my cultures. An entire dress had never been made with embroidered lace, but I like challenges; with fourteen women and three and a half months of work we pulled it off. I've made shoes of gold, corsets with Murano glass, wooden purses, wicker jackets and skirts, and porcelain hats, first of all to satisfy the desire to infuse fashion with a little artisanal craft, and secondly to succeed in doing the impossible. I even tracked down a costumer who had worked with Fellini to make illuminated pieces to be presented with the Fall–Winter 1999– 2000 collection. Anything is possible if you really want it!

When you create your models do you think of an ideal woman and design for her, or is it a matter of a woman who changes each season?

S/S 2000

I like obstinate women, who are aware of their own grace and femininity, but who also fully realize that they're just as strong as men, if not more so. My clothes are not meant for an insignificant woman, but for one who holds her own destiny and good qualities tightly in hand. It's a type of woman who could change her taste each season, but, as they say, a leopard never changes its spots. I think that my sister Piera embodies all these aspects: she's perhaps the most elegant woman I know, my most enthusiastic fan, and my most severe critic. I always ask her opinion of what I do, and I unconditionally admire her—she's taught me a lot.

Are there people, events, or moments of your childhood that let you know you would become a fashion designer?

We grew up aware of the importance of clothing and personal care. I remember when I was five or six years old and I would go to London from Lincolnshire with my brother and father to try on our customized suits; or when, with my mother, we bought suits for the trip to Sicily (back then you dressed up to travel). In Lincolnshire we were the only foreigners for miles around, and we were always the best dressed. I grew up with a passion for clothes, and began to buy them when I was nine: that was my first Armani sweater, with leather appliqués knotted onto the shoulders, which cost me 110 pound sterling (twenty-one years ago that was a pretty sum). It was then that I realized I wanted to be a fashion designer. I also liked to go to church; I come from a very religious family and during our stays in Sicily going to mass was obligatory. The church wasn't only exteriority and ceremony (Sicilians like anything that is a little baroque), but also fun and games and a meeting point for all the kids in Bivana (billiards, soccer, card games, you played everything in the sacristy!). I remember once I had to be the altar boy and I had put on the tunic, which seemed fantastic. Unfortunately, though, my friends and cousins weren't of the same opinion, so I never participated in the procession; but I kept the cleric's tunic on.

Did moving to Italy somehow change your way of working, and, if so, how?

I think that I am growing here. London is all ideas, models to exhibit, and sceneries that prevail over the content; in Italy you do business and above all clothes. It won't be as exciting, everyone will say, but for me it's certainly more stimulating, because I begin to question my self, my ideas, and my

F/W 1999–2000

S/S 2000

decisions. What models to exhibit is one thing, but industrially producing them in such a way as to make them more portable and easier are factors that I'm beginning to consider equally fundamental. I know that the pieces for the catwalk are important because ideas can find their expression in fashion, but clothing is made to be worn and appreciated, and sometimes the "exhibition piece" dresses, so difficult to create, are easily laid aside. A balance is necessary.

How does the Italian public seem to you?

It's more difficult to satisfy. In Italy there aren't just models, but everything is supermodels, celebrity and, even more importantly, advertising. People

F/W 1999–2000

F/W 1999–2000

applaud Naomi or Eva regardless of what they have on, because it's them. On top of that, Italian journalists don't have a real background in fashion, they want press releases and gossip, the fashion show itself interests them little; more than anything else they want to write their piece. In England they let anyone in, students, fans, and anyone who just passes by, while in Italy you can't do that for security reasons, so there are times when the enthusiasm is absolutely nonexistent. Aside from that, I like to be here.

Kammi advertising campaign

Missoni advertising campaign

Mario Valentino advertising campaign

Gucci advertising campaign

ALLURING, SENSUAL, BURNING, AT TIMES PATENTLY EXPLICIT—THE METAPHOR OF SEX FOR SALE IN THE ADVERTISING IMAGERY THAT LEADS DOWN THE ROAD TO ENTICEMENT.

by FAUSTO CALETTI

STEP BY STEP

ADVERTISING'S ROAD TO ENTICEMENT

BOTTEGA VENETA

Ever since the time of primitive costumes sex and clothing have gone hand in hand; but as winter begins to melt into spring one notes a blatant reference to sex for sale. Fashion advertising is a veritable homage to prostitution. We were unaccustomed to such intentioned women; the minimalist years had imposed an emaciated and ambiguously perverse sexuality. Only on television did the woman-prostitute exist, thanks to the constant presence of pretty young things in undies and push-up bras; but fashion had removed the iconography of sex for sale. Today a showy, elegantly decked out woman has returned, with all the erotic decoys right where they should be.

This is not a new topic, it's enough to go back to 1971: for the Spring–Summer collection Yves

LE VERE PUTTANE
SONO GLI UOMINI.

SWISH JEAN

ISH JEANS

LOVE
SEX
MONEY

FOUR SEASONS HOTEL

MILANO

DAL 27 SETTEMBRE

AL 3 OTTOBRE

Saint Laurent hearkened back to the 1940s and offered up short fox furs, sandals with solid heels, and turbans; every fashion journalist wrote that women don't want to look like prostitutes, even high-end ones. Saint Laurent had always found inspiration on the streets, and with this retro reference he began to load his fashion with ever more explicit meanings. Two years later creative types went back to that col-lection, and every chic woman explicitly exhib-ited herself, ready to be approached. In the 1980s the bitch-lady triumphed, from the trash icons of *Dallas* and *Dynasty*—heroines always ready to go to bed with anyone out of conve-nience—to fashion. Jean-Paul Gaultier and Claude Montana proposed prostitutes of every sort, from sadomasochistic to retro, and Lagerfeld, for both Chanel and his own line, was

STEVEN KLEIN

Alexander McQueen Eyes advertising campaign

7/19/00 5:47:31

212

mcqueen eyes
www.alexandermcqueen.net

Jeannot

collectionautumnwinter'00/'01

MILONA

one long homage to slut style. Models of the period suffered through not only super-heavy makeup and hairstyling, but they even strode the catwalk flailing purses to the spanking rhythm of their thighs. In the early 1990s Gianni Versace and Dolce & Gabbana propagandized

the pin-up girl that soon came close to being a trailer park transvestite. Versace himself declared, "I create clothes for the women who attract men with functioning hormones."

Another slut lover was Franco Moschino, who replied to those who denigrated him for his ele-

zooi

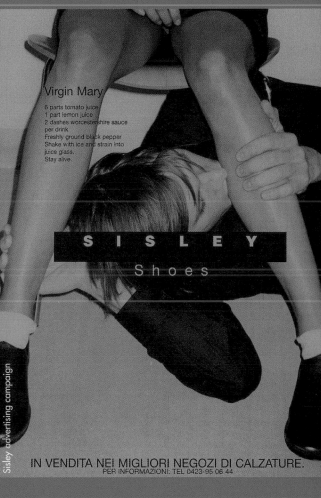

Virgin Mary

6 parts tomato juice
1 part lemon juice
2 dashes worcestershire sauce
per drink
Freshly ground black pepper
Shake with ice and strain into
juice glass.
Stay alive.

SISLEY
Shoes

IN VENDITA NEI MIGLIORI NEGOZI DI CALZATURE.
PER INFORMAZIONI: TEL 0423-95 06 44

gantly vulgar vein by saying, "The faux prostitutes that I send down the catwalk are less vulgar than some of the women you find walking
around offices." And then the void; the 1990s
were an ode to perverse sexuality, but in fashion imagery everyone kept their distance from
references to sex for sale. In 1997, anyway,
Alexander McQueen for Givenchy and John
Galliano for Dior both invented défilé that
shocked: the former with a street and street-
lamps, the latter with a brothel setting, they
exhibited a bewitching woman, more explicit

Miu Miu advertising campaign

miu miu
Corso Venezia - Milano
Via Roma 62 - Firenze

Dior advertising campaign

Dior

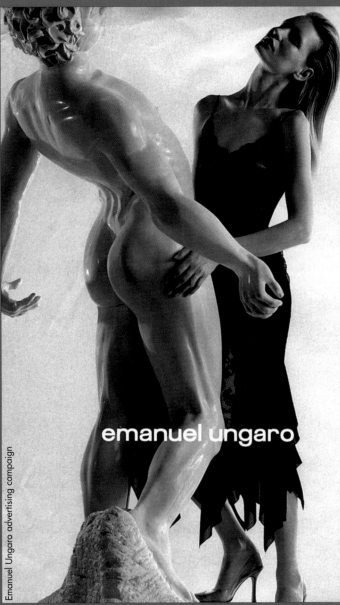

Emanuel Ungaro advertising campaign

emanuel ungaro

than ever. The two collections were an ode to slut chic; groin-exposing miniskirts, vertiginous heels, anatomical silhouettes, big hair, heavy makeup, and animal-prints completed by purses and trinkets signaled the end of the minimal style. In 2000 Cavalli, the fashion designer who

in the last few seasons has brought together all possible alluring fetishes, triumphed.
So the slut is nothing new, but is the nth revival that fashion has nurtured in order to renew itself and reaffirm that elegance really is something else altogether.

OPIUM
le parfum par
YvesSaintLaurent

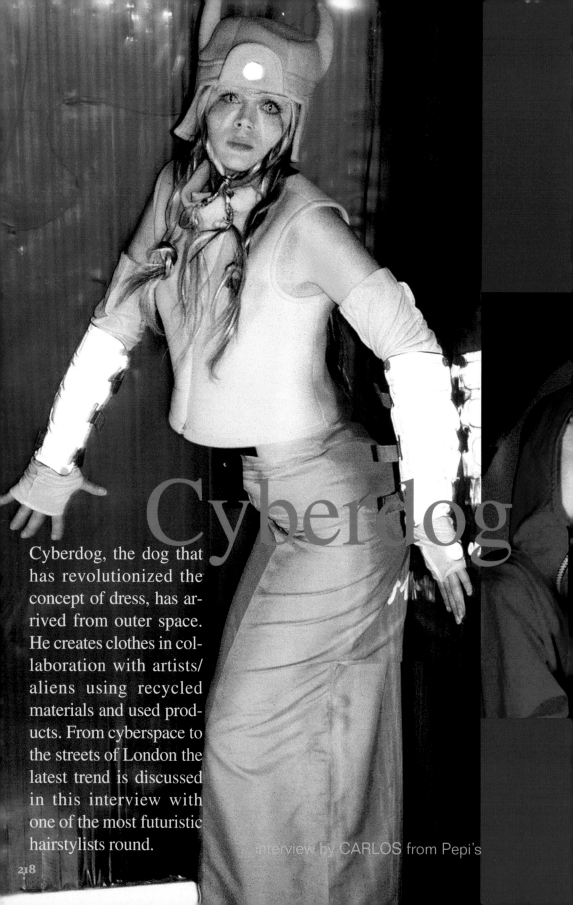

Cyberdog

Cyberdog, the dog that has revolutionized the concept of dress, has arrived from outer space. He creates clothes in collaboration with artists/aliens using recycled materials and used products. From cyberspace to the streets of London the latest trend is discussed in this interview with one of the most futuristic hairstylists round.

interview by CARLOS from Pepi's

Carlos: Why did you start designing clothes?

Cyberdog: Cyberdog is our leader: we're just its terrestrial executors.

Do you remember the first thing you made and were proud of?

Cyberdog wanted a dog collar that would function as an alarm clock after wild nights. At the time we were novices in this game of realizing its desires, and we didn't really get the concept; so we designed a t-shirt with a penis-shaped alien! Nothing too intelligent, nothing to be proud of . . . but it sure made us laugh.

How and when did you start?

About five years ago we were waiting at the bus stop and we saw a flash of light. Cyberdog appeared, belched, and the rest is history.

Did you encounter much resistance in the fashion world, since you didn't come from some prestigious fashion or design institute?

I wouldn't say that Cyberdog conforms to many British fashion standards, and clearly it didn't have any support to help affirm its validity. It had no intention to follow the trends just to please others in the field; Cyberdog was sent with the mission to always be on the cutting edge in the evolu-

tion of fashion, and has never wavered. It chose to be the fashion design-er of a "street/club fashion," for people it cares about: the youth (even if only at heart), young progressives sick and tired of reliving the past through "retro," the survivors of the binge of consumerism in the 1980s who now look ahead, to the future. "Clubwear" wasn't considered true fashion until even the best designers got behind it! Perhaps Cyberdog didn't attend the right schools in the field of fashion, but it's traveled in cyberspace with eyes wide open; sticks and stones may break your bones, but if you're a cybernetic dog with a savage virus you couldn't care less!

Almost all the designers produce two collections twice a year. "Haute couture" and "prêt-à-porter": the former is excessive, uncomfortable, and not easily worn, at exorbitant prices; the second is accessible, without personality, highly commercial, and cynical. You're not of that same mold, but how do you manage to remain creative and innovative without switching your cuffs and pant legs? How do you manage, in other words, to keep a balance?

Mold? Perhaps I moved too slowly and Cyberdog wanted to run, not walk. Keeping a balance is a necessary reality for surviving in this world, but everything depends on your motivations. In Cyberdog's case the mission is—and has always been—very clear: don't let yourself be ruled by money, as proved by the fact that its clothes have something very non-commercial about them and the label is still considered underground. On the other hand it doesn't want to be a presumptuous idiot, hence the more accessible models; in this sense it's perhaps similar to other designers, but does it on a much smaller scale. What Cyberdog avoids above all is allowing the label to prevaricate, and it doesn't expect its customers to buy any old pair of pants with its name on them just to see their butt wiggle round behind it; it's not progressive, and that's decidedly not its scope. At the beginning Cyberdog aimed to offer clothing that wasn't readily available just anywhere, that was progressive but wearable, and its ethics haven't changed over time. So cuffs and pant legs won't be discontinued.

Where would you like to take Cyberdog?

To the park!

Why don't you ever use your names when dealing with the media?

Cyberdog is the brain, but it's very shy; so we speak in its place. At the end of the day who wants glory? Behind Cyberdog there is a team that does whatever it wants. The compensation lies in seeing people have fun wearing the clothes and interpret them in their own way. They don't need a pat on the back, but a scratch behind the ears would be welcome.

Your stores have a lot of style: installations, works of art, cafés, cutting edge music. Is it all the work of Cyberdog or do you have the help of collaborators? How is it all born?

The stores are the true mirror of Cyberdog, with a few approximations that are quite far from being clinically unexceptionable. Cyberdog wants the stores to represent the "future" that we're now living in, dangerous and exciting but far from being perfect. The idea is that going to its stores can be a way of having fun and that they give the sensation of escape, but not in a virtual way—the same sensation that you get when you enter a bustling club with music at full volume; music is the determining factor for the stores' atmosphere. Cyberdog wants people to walk around and enjoy themselves as much as possible. A lot of people don't want to grow up and they flee from mass approval, but they want to have fun, and who ever said that you can't have fun shopping? Certainly not Cyberdog. But the most important goal is, in any case, to offer a space in which people can take a break, dance, observe, and relax; this is what we call shopping! The furnishing and interior design of the stores is the product of collaboration between Cyberdog and characters/artists who share the same feelings. They're perfectly free to express themselves. Many of the interactive installations were designed by Vincent Jones, another Alien Artist, who has fun using leftover junk. Most of the furnishings and designs are actually created with recycled materials or products used in ways they weren't originally meant to be. And all of it put together has made a nice jumble!

Can you give us a peek at the future jeans, underwear, or perfumes of Cyberdog?

What a silly idea! Right now in the collections there are some denim models (not true jeans). Underwear? Well, hopefully with some of these garments you can also go to bed. Perfume? That makes me think of dog shit. Who knows? Laugh if you want, but if Cyberdog has gone to a place that inspired it to produce toxic waste in a bottle and electrically charged underwear, maybe that's just what he's done. So, if what you're looking for are men's boxer briefs that open at the front, you'd be better off going to Calvin Klein!

Thierry Mugler

Thierry Mugler. Photo Dominique Issermann

"Humor in fashion is not something just of this century; it existed in the extravagant hats of Marie Antoinette, in the *à la girafe* hairstyles of the Restoration . . . Humor is timeless, universal. I need it in order to live, like I need water, love, and salt . . ." Former ballet dancer, fascinated by theater and the glamour of divas throughout history, Thierry Mugler is without a doubt one of the greatest creators of fashion who has chosen the idiom of hybridization.

by FAUSTO CALETTI

Jerry Hall in White Sands. Photo Thierry Mugler, 1995

The close relationship between fashion and theater, and the simple fact that theater is considered apace with fashion, is the access code necessary for understanding the work of Thierry Mugler. His first fashion show dates back to 1977, and since then he has explored every possible artifice. His woman could dress as an insect, robot, flower, or cartoon character, but she will always remain a woman of great fashion, capable of "finding a lot of men to fuck," as Mugler affirms during his appearance in Altman's film *Prêt-à-porter.* Often the spasmodic search of special effects for his presentations runs the risk of distracting from the beauty of his dresses, or could pass as simply a way of confusing people; but Mugler manages to balance provocation with the technique of a master tailor. Idolized by an infinite number of women because he succeeds in giving femininity even to those who haven't any whatsoever, he often has fun minimizing the limits between body and dress, creating every sort of hybrid imaginable; each outfit is structured in such a way as to exist as an independent body, in a marked ambiguity between reality and appearance. For Mugler subverting the three sociological fundamentals of fashion—modesty, protection, and ornament—becomes the only possibility for seeing creation, considered the constant fusion of calculated perversion and the trans-human trend. His search knows no bounds: in 1985 he was the first to use the fashion of the 1970s; in 1989 he was the first to believe in fetish fashion; in 1992 he was the first to create a perfume made of cocoa, an edible perfume (*Angel*); and he was the absolute first to make steel heels. In 1992 it was fetishism that drove him toward another artistic mode of expression, causing him to direct George Michael's music video *Too Funky*, a bona fide manifesto of Mugler's thought; a group of supermodels struts through fire, walking sexily and magnetically, and stride forward, transformed in "Muglerettes," sexy cyberheroines made in Hollywood.

The ironic winking between sex and fashion is infinite, and is only the beginning: already in 1982 Thierry Mugler dedicated his collection to Minnie, who goes to Hollywood; in 1988 he concentrated on vamped-up vampires who yell, "Gothic Velvet"; and the following season was the shift of the sexy sirens of Atlantis. In 1990 he changed woman into a well-molded *roulée comme une Buick*, in 1992 into a "pin-up/cowgirl," and for the Winter 1998 season he made her wear garters, predicting the crescendo of couturiers' bravado and spectacular advertising catalogues. Image is so important for him that toward the mid-1980s he began to personally take the photographs of his creations. This marked the beginning of an unlimited search for scenographic sets, from Paris to the desert, from New York to Moscow; he superimposed the models onto these backdrops, transforming them into ice-cold, perverse, frivolous superwomen. His photographs are an ode to gigantism, and raise the subject to the status of a pagan divinity. His perennial play with the female body is the cue for not working only on the clothes, but also on the makeup, hairstyling, and everything comes together to become and integral part of his creation. It is typical of Mugler to consider clothing a second skin, or an exoskeleton that transforms woman into a sexy robot. To underline his way of conceiving fashion fused with theater, in 1995 he celebrated twenty years of career with a fashion show including the best of his collections, all worn by

F/W 1997–1998. Photo Thierry Orban

famous people. Very different women participated in the event: Jerry Hall and Darryl Hannah, the Kessler twins and Amanda Lear, transvestites and transsexuals, leading up to the delicious seventy-year-old Carmen Dell'Orefice; the thing these women had in common was the spicy attraction of Mugler. In 1995, for her *Human Nature* music video, he also dressed Madonna, the queen of stylistic transformation, with one of his classics—a vinyl cat suit and steel-heeled boots. In 1997 Mugler became a true couturier and presented his first haute couture collection. Famous for his super-structured suits, on occasion of this presentation he ignored all expectations with outfits that were completely different from his classics, which mark the bust-waist-hips points, creating teardrop-shaped volumes. About two seasons ago he invented a white suit that starts from the models' two nipple piercings, another first in fetish couture. With his magic touch everything becomes a provocation, regardless, even the most chaste of dresses. All of his creations are characterized by irony and frivolousness. King of artifice, sorcerer of attraction, for over twenty-five years Thierry Mugler has dressed women in erotic dreams and provocative promises, always with the lightness typical to one who lives without false taboos.

Robot Couture, Cirque d'Hiver, 1995

228

Second-skin dresses, strategic zippers that diagonally slice the silhouette, tattoo effects, and diagonal seams; the idea that Azzedine Alaïa has of femininity is a mixture of refinement, charm, and detachment. His sexy dresses are never exhibitionist, and end up appearing hieratic. For Alaïa a dress serves only to make a woman feel at ease, and make her beautiful without betraying her trust.

Azzedine Alaïa with Tina Turner, Paris, 1995. Photo Peter Lindbergh

Azzedine Alaïa

by FAUSTO CALETTI

229

At the end of the 1970s fashion victims had a choice between the newborn Italian prêt-à-porter or the sought-after transgressive classics of Yves Saint Laurent; there were very few voices outside these lines, and the most important of these was represented by the style of Azzedine Alaïa. His first all-black collection shocked both the public and press with the aggressive force of its sexy style trimmed with punk references. In 1981 Bill Cunningham, the mythic American photographer, got Alaïa's dresses into *Women's Wear Daily*, and it exploded into an instant success. In the United States everyone went crazy for his layered, highly structured, and yet so essential dresses. The typical Alaïa silhouette dates back to these years, with important shoulders, a slim waist, seams just above the kneecap, and high heels. In 1982 he presented his collection in New York, and beat all sales records for an emerging fashion designer. America didn't know that Alaïa had been working since 1957, the year he moved to Paris, for Dior and soon thereafter for Laroche. His apprenticeship with these giants became his technical foundation, and he always created his garments personally, without the aid of assistants and modelers. Later on he worked for Thierry Mugler. His need to invent everything from the model on pushes Alaïa beyond the second-skin dresses; his creations always have something more. In the early 1980s he invented silhouettes pierced by strategically placed zippers skewed to slice the dress diagonally, as if they were an orange peel. These diagonal zips, which soon became emblematic of his style, are for him the modern reprise of an Arletty dress—the 1930s and 1940s cinema diva Alaïa venerated. Arletty, who was called the "perfect one" of chic Parisian style, was the inspiring muse for him, so much so that in the 1960s he did any and everything in order to meet her. At the time he dressed Cecile de Rothschild and Greta Garbo, who represented the idea that Azzedine had of femininity; refinement, charm, and a certain detachment. The magic of his dresses is that, while they are sexy, they are never exhibitionist; actually, they often end up appearing hieratic. Knitwear and leather are Alaïa's favorite materials, perhaps because of the opposing nature of their peculiarities, as knitwear is soft and flexible, while leather is structured and robust. These extremisms are typical of

Azzedine Alaïa with Madonna, *Vogue Italia*, Paris, 1989. Photo Steven Meisel

his style, and finding harmony in contrast is, for Alaïa, a way of making women express themselves. He always declares that a dress serves only to make a woman feel at ease, placing her personality and face in high relief, in other words, to render her beautiful without betraying her trust. In 1983 he opened his first boutique on Rodeo Drive in Beverly Hills, and in the same period Tina Turner was photographed wearing his dresses, and enamored of his style. Tina wanted to meet Azzedine, who, very flattered, went on to dress her in several music videos; Madonna and Diana Ross also wear Alaïa in their private lives. These were the years in which he invented exasperatingly form-fitting silhouettes. Alaïa suits and blouses became status symbols, as did the

S/S 1987 . Photo Jean-Baptiste Mondino

dresses created from cut-up jerseys. His international success was so great that in 1985 the Museum of Modern Art in Bordeaux presented a retrospective of his work. The years in which, in his tiny atelier, Azzedine took care even of customer sales—personally advising them to lose a little paunch before wearing a particular style, or to choose a color that would bring out their physical features—were long gone. For the Spring–Summer 1986 collection he invented the slip dress, redefining a classic from the 1930s in homage to Grès and Madame Vionnet. This last fashion designer, master of the bias cut and draping, together with Charles James, magician of the architectonic cut in dresses, were the two largest references for Alaïa. Perhaps in order to emulate Charles James, who according to legend could lose up to four years structuring the perfect sleeve, Alaïa stopped presenting his collections during the prêt-à-porter calendar toward the end of the 1980s. A crowd of fans followed him anyway, and the French edition of *Elle* dedicated a special issue

Grace Jones, F/W 1987–1988. Photo Martine Barrat

to his collection every six months. The pace of fashion won't do for this sophisticated artist of the cut. In the early 1990s his creations were still sensational. In 1991 he decided to utilize the maxi-plaid of Vichy, trademark of Tati, the largest and cheapest warehouse store of Paris, for his prêt-à-porter collection. *Vogue* dedicated a major article to him in which he posed with Jasmine Ghuari, the top supermodel of the period. For Winter 1991–1992 he invented a wholly "leopardized" fashion show immortalized by the lens of Herb Ritts and worn by Naomi Campbell. The following year he offered cat suits and tattoo effects, decidedly at the cutting edge of the era. During these years his passion is focused exclusively on the tricot; because of this in 1996 the group Linea Più, one of the world's largest and most powerful yarn and thread producers, curated an exhibition dedicated to Alaïa's work at Palazzo Corsini in Florence. In a beautiful installation, the dresses were worn by Plexiglas mannequins, each molded according to the profile of the dress, and Alaïa exhibited his mastery of couture constructions. Each garment seemed simple, hid preformed cups that emphasized the bust, and had technical elaborations that transformed the threads into nearly sculptural works. And yet this little Tunisian gentleman, perennially dressed in a uniform and black Chinese slippers, declares that he dresses women that want nothing other than to appear, simply, beautiful beyond what they are wearing.

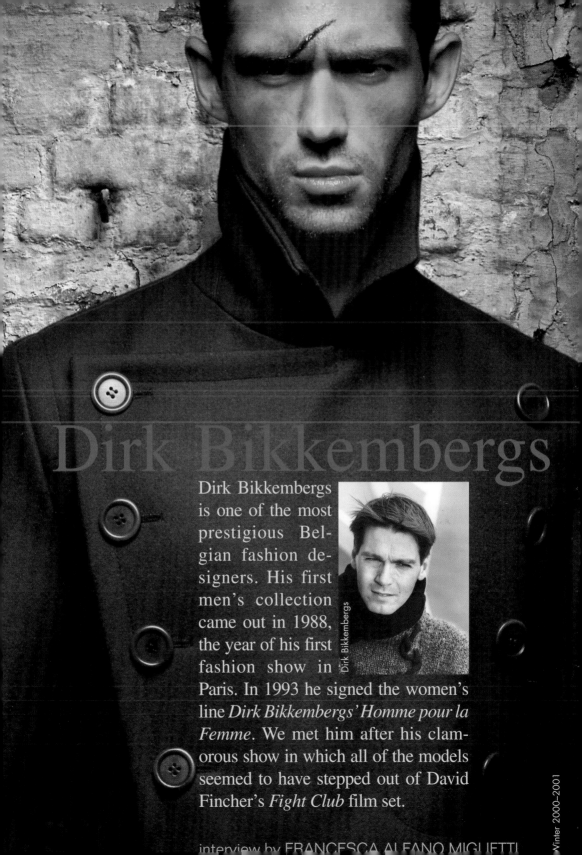

Dirk Bikkembergs

Dirk Bikkembergs is one of the most prestigious Belgian fashion designers. His first men's collection came out in 1988, the year of his first fashion show in Paris. In 1993 he signed the women's line *Dirk Bikkembergs' Homme pour la Femme*. We met him after his clamorous show in which all of the models seemed to have stepped out of David Fincher's *Fight Club* film set.

Dirk Bikkembergs

interview by FRANCESCA ALFANO MIGLIETTI

Francesca Alfano Miglietti: Is there a particular type of body you think of when you design?

Dirk Bikkembergs: I think of a healthy, athletic, high-tech body, and I often think of the body as a geometric structure that expresses pure energy.

Do you believe that in the future the body will continue to choose the universe of mutation?

Yes, the human body is in continual metamorphosis and I think that it will continue to mutate like this just as the sensuality that it unleashes mutates! It is a game of prestige between its energy and controlling the tension that it produces and emanates.

What difference is there for you between "evolution" and "mutation"?

Evolution is always positive, and mutation doesn't always have to be! Perhaps because we've always thought evolution is a "natural phenomenon" and mutation is a form of "self-changing." The positive/negative sign is transformed from time to time, according to how much a social reality impacts individual change. Everything around us is becoming a McDonald's product: made, packaged, served, consumed. I think all that has more to do with mutation than with evolution!

Contusions, bruises, cuts, wounds . . . the models of your Winter 2000–2001 men's collection seem to expose the traces of a combat just barely sustained. Are you indicating a new model of seduction that comes to us through the signs of strength and force?

Our reality is a violent one, a situation that expresses conflict in multiple forms. The idea that the concept of boredom stimu-

Winter 2000–2001

lates the brain is unbearable. Everything that surrounds us in reality hides the void of emotions and the incapacity to relate with civility to others. Physical pain is an emotional vehicle that overflows into many manifestations of the contemporary: tattoos, piercings, branding, lesions, cuts, wounds of all sorts. My models have simply amplified this type of tension. I don't produce forms of violence, actually, all told, I think of athletic and active bodies, but in any case of bodies that live in the contemporary; the fact that these bodies carry the signs of the violence that surrounds them seemed to have major impact.

The women you've had in your latest collections' shows seem to be hybrids between the human and the artificial. What relationship is there between the "human" bodies you choose and the "bodies" of your creation?

Once again the answer lies in the difference between evolution and mutation; the woman I imagine when I design lives a life that mirrors the current world, in which all that is feminine becomes always less so with respect to the classic canons. I don't know if the new type of feminine beauty passes for artificial, certainly resorting to manipulating practices is always more widespread. Anyway, I choose living models, not bodies I have made for me in the laboratory!

All your clothes hybridize distant cultures among themselves; do you think that hybridization can be a chance?

Always! The most beautiful flowers are always born from hybridization.

The Winter collections you have designed show very undressed bodies. What does the exposure of the body represent for you?

Nature, truth, simplicity, pain and pleasure—basically, life! The body's movement and its expression represent the beginning of my inspiration.

Does fashion, according to you, design clothing or new corporeal spheres?

It depends on who's watching and how they're watching. The interpretation of the clothing itself changes from person to person. For me it's not the clothes that make the man, but the man that makes

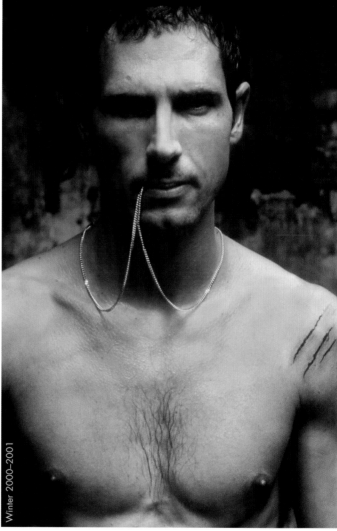

Winter 2000–2001

the clothes; I believe strongly in the individuality of the person. Fashion for me is a form of expression that needs to be understood, loved, cultivated, and appreciated. Like for the majority of creative expressions, also for fashion interpretation is not a marginal factor but a consistent part of its whole meaning. Thus clothing can be a simple, recombined fabric or a corporeal frontier . . . it depends on a series of factors, not least on who wears it!

Monica

Hair and makeup artist, after a long period working in New York Monica Coppola returned to Milan to collaborate with her father, Aldo Coppola, on the creation of calendars and art books for L'Oréal. In 1998 she began

Coppola

to invent and realize a new way of presenting the fashion trends in hairstyling, creating shows and events that tend to provide evidence of the contaminations and hybridizations between genres and cultures.

interview by FAM

Aldo Coppola, Twins, Vogue Italia, 1993. Photo Fabrizio Ferri

FAM: Father and daughter . . . an idyll, intrigue, ring, set, game, match . . . What is it for you?

Monica Coppola: "Fathers" and "daughters" are not categories, but a singular, unique relationship—for everyone a story in itself. I have learned a lot from him, above all by watching him. Between us there is a crazy competition that forced me to learn to watch and look beyond initial appearances. My father is not a tame person, nor am I; we both had to learn, beyond any affection, to respect and appreciate one another for what each of us two isn't, and what the other is.

From the moon to fairytales, from clones to cyborgs—these are images of women in a vision that tends to create dreamed-of or imaginary identities realized in the present. What, for you, is identity?

My conception of identity is very similar to the reality expressed by the Australian Aborigines in Wim Wenders' *Until the End of the World*. For me identity is not a daytime one, but that of dreams, of all the dreams that we have ever dreamed since we were born up to today. The women you see in these images are all the women that I myself am; I try to live all the identities that each one of us dreams, I live them and I let them be born inside and outside of me, as images, forms, icons, as traces of a reality that exists beyond the rigidity of the rational. I think it's a little like in Robinson's *What Dreams May Come*; each of us, when we die, go into our dreams. I am convinced that hell is the lack of dreams.

What stimulates you the most—cinema, travel, meeting people, music . . .?

All this put together, but absolutely travel and trips are my personal way of bringing about self-transformation. I have never been a "tourist"; for me trips are sensorial empowerment, I seek out places and encounters that show me how to open my eyes and see more clearly and at the same time to close them and dream other dreams. I always leave without a hardened shell, because while traveling I don't need to protect myself, but rather to abandon myself. That is the only way for my eyes to see, my ears to hear, and my hands to touch.

What difference is there between costume and fashion?

A costume is a way to tell a particular, temporal, singular episode, and it is one of the signals of the Zeitgeist. There was a time not so long ago when even fashion was part of costume. Today perhaps fashion has been made banal in a superficial attempt to describe people, a sort of "dressing" of anonymous individuals who give themselves an identity accepted by the world they live in. Why is it that in the eighteenth and nineteenth centuries costume identified itself with fashion and today no longer does? Today people experience their identities like a mask, well-dressed masks—more precisely, the mask of fashion. Fashion right now is a long, popular illustrated novel for everyday people in which excerpts of other people's films parade through the plot.

Hair has become more than ever one of the bodily territories where mutation is a daily practice, as is the search for new morphological combinations.

What is it for you, aside from the raw material for your creations?

Hair is the part of you that keeps you connected to your childhood. I think that through hair one can identify character. Hair is a living part of the human body: it is born, it grows, it breaks, it falls out after a stressful shock . . . It is one of the body's visible, living parts that participates in your emotional life, but also a distinguishing part from a political, religious, and social point of view. Think of Islamic cultures: hair has to be covered, while in other cultures it is shaved off. From a social point of view, in the 1960s people grew it out as a rebellion against a lifestyle they refused. But hair is also one of the "places" of the body where violence is done; collaborationist women were shaved, and in concentration camps hair was also eliminated . . . Coco Chanel launched the image of a woman who takes back her own life by cutting her hair and taking off her bustier—two emblems of a constricted, subjected, external femininity.

Extensions and grafts—what are the materials you work with most?

I work a lot with real hair, hair from Chinese or Thai women who let it grow out in order to then sell it; and I feel the histories of this hair, histories that speak of poor women who strip themselves of some parts of their beauty . . . But I prefer to work with artificial hair and more alien materials like plastic, flowers, metal mesh screens, all the materials that are a part of our daily life.

What relationship is there between the natural and the artificial in your work?

My work is completely artificial; I am the natural element. In the end I find the border between the two idioms of very little interest; they are not opposites, but are by now closely intertwined. Is a film natural or artificial?

What is your "secret" project?

My secret project is the communication through a series of stimuli, a way of being able to transmit the possibility of becoming a central part of one's own existence. I have no sympathy for gurus and life coaches, but do for sensations and forms and projects that teach seeing and feeling . . . This is a moment in which everyone thinks they can realize their own "project"; my project is a silence in which one can listen to whispers and breaths, and in which, after the blinding light, one will be able to discern the luminescent contour of shadow.

Aldo and Monica Coppola by Fabrizio Ferri, L'Oréal calendar *No Time*, 1999–2000

From the *C'era una volta* catalogue, 1996, L'Oréal. Photo Javier Vallhonrat, courtesy of Coppola Agency

243

Jeremy Scott

Jeremy Scott is the hot new name in the eye of the storm of the international fashion world. Isabella Blow, the "Fashion Saint," is his inspiring muse. Skin and Björk are the incarnation of his type of woman; a sublime, perversely sophisticated creature of ice-cold sensuality.

by FAUSTO CALETTI

Is it possible to become a fashion icon in less than three years' time?
Certainly, if your name is Jeremy Scott.
Not quite thirty years old, and a native of Kansas City, Jeremy studied at the Pratt Institute in New York. The orientation of his style is spiked and hard, but glamorous, with a very cutting edge couture taste—so much so that he himself wrote "vive l'avant-garde" in red spray paint on last season's sleeveless tees, making the ultimate statement.
With the scrawl of a New York graffiti artist, the emaciated face of a hardened clubber, and a twiggy, ill-looking body, Jeremy Scott appears as a character straight out of *Desperately Seeking Susan*. This continual reference to the 1980s is the constant inspiration of all his work.
In 1997 his very first fashion show, "only for the happy few," was a re-reading of the geometric dresses, redone and refinished with strategic zippers;

Body Modification, 1996

glacial sensuality. On the other hand, he shares with McQueen the presence of Isabella Blow, who does his PR and is his inspiring muse, the fashion saint who immediately took him under her powerfully protective wing. Only a year later Jeremy presented a fashion show in grand form entitled *Rich White Women*. It was a shiver-inspiring show, and presented impalpable, all-enveloping ensembles atop super-high heels that avoided the use of regular shoes by lacing the heel directly to the models' ankles—the foot remained as if magically suspended. The image of lightness reached its height when plissé forms resembling angel's wings or immaterial seashells wrapped around the models came onto the catwalk.

The collection circled the world and was immediately noticed for its freshness and the perfection of the cuts. One of the most notable models asymmetrically unified a miniskirt and pant leg. The insignias of the Winter 1998–1999 collection were gold and geometric form—themes taken, as always, from the 1980s. Jeremy Scott has fun creating so-called fashion designer's clothes; goofy, unthinkable, ironic—in a word, provocative. Last year's Spring–Summer collection was a delirium of tight minidresses made of leather sewn into intarsia, black and white, super sturdy, trimmed in gold profiles and sealed with minute tassels, just as in the consumer-crazed 1980s. His archetypal woman reached her apotheosis: a small head with hair tightly pulled back, heavily lined eyes, and fire red lips, just like in the decade of the power suit. Scott reached his apex posing for his own ads, surrounded by models with incendiary mouths and black dresses with gigantic shoulders; in the group photographs, which look as though they were stolen from a famous music video by Robert Palmer, the phrase "life is a dream" camps out, scrawled in bright red lipstick. Life really has turned into a dream for Jeremy, even if, since he was a little kid, he always knew he would become a star. For the Winter 1999–2000 season came yet another change in style; the fashion world is invaded by neo-hippies, and he reinvents the conservative, but tinged with shocking pink. The cult magazine *Visionaire* dedicated whole pages to him as the symbolic epitome of the newfound, eccentric, and flashy luxury making a comeback after a decade of raw minimalism. For Jeremy the best icon is Linda Evans in *Dynasty*, and his silhouette composed of impeccable garments seems perfect for her: ruffle-trimmed blouses, straight pants, fox furs, and knee-length skirts—the look of a true lady, but neon pink. And it's precisely on the wave of neo-bon-ton that his Spring–Summer 2000 season brings

Rich White Women, 1998

Body Modification, 1996

back safe beige suits, impeccable trench coats, and diaphanous dresses in multicolored chiffon. The season was given an ironic touch with his proposal of dresses and purses with a fabric that obsessively repeats the logo "Jeremy Scott Paris," like those of the historic fashion houses.

The same game was brought to the table again this winter: almost classic silhouettes in the most bourgeois color possible—Hermes orange. The fashion gag is embodied in his gigantic scrawls of "Paris" that camp out on his sweaters and pullovers. Naturally the writings are backwards, as if seen in a mirror, just to reconfirm that the meaning of his style goes far beyond what it seems.

His brief but brilliant career includes collaborations with important names (in 1998 he was called by Trussardi to be appointed artistic director), friendships with international stars (Björk and Skin often wear his clothes), and portraits with the most celebrated names of fashion design (even Karl Lagerfeld has posed with him). The hot new name in the eye of the storm of the international fashion world, in his explosive career he has already succeeded in inventing a style that has become a status symbol. What more can he do? A whole lot more—after all, his name is Jeremy Scott.

Rich White Women, 1998

United Aliens

United Aliens is an "artistic collective" founded by Roberto O Heinrichsen, who claims, "In fashion we always produce useless articles." United Aliens invites us to confront a world in which the frontiers between art, means of mass communication, digital images, fashion, film, and graphics have begun to dissolve their borders.

interview by FAM

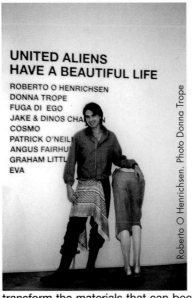

UNITED ALIENS
HAVE A BEAUTIFUL LIFE
ROBERTO O HENRICHSEN
DONNA TROPE
FUGA DI EGO
JAKE & DINOS CHA...
COSMO
PATRICK O'NEIL
ANGUS FAIRHU...
GRAHAM LITTL...
EVA

Roberto O Henrichsen. Photo Donna Trope

We are the components of a team whose primary objective deals with forms of expression, and in particular all the idioms that generate and inspire forms of spiritual wellbeing. Our project integrates fashion philosophy, art, and media. Our ethos could be compared to that of an alchemist. We call into being and transform the materials that can become conceptual, visual, or pragmatic in order to funnel the magic of the product (our exchange of energy) into a form of purity and beauty. (Patrick O'Neil, United Aliens)

FAM: Where do these aliens come from?

Roberto O Henrichsen: No one knows whether they're from another planet or this planet, which is the most alien of all . . . Even today there are still no sure data about our origin as a species; sometimes I get the feeling that we appeared on the planet already civilized . . . When I was little in Rio de Janeiro I saw with my own eyes a very large sphere of light. At first it stood still and was very visible, then it began to make some very fast movements, and it entered and exited terrestrial space like a comet. Often I get the feeling that humans are only guests on this planet, and they do not behave, and have not behaved, very well, given the disastrous results we see . . .

What is the philosophy of United Aliens based on?

All of our work is centered on "waking up": we propose a form of spiritual awareness, no longer a material awareness. Up until now we had thought that the secret of happiness were a material evolution, but now it is necessary to unite as a single people, no longer divided by political states, with the awareness and irony that we are all terrestrials, and not simply Americans or Germans or English or Africans . . . The races will mix themselves more and more, and I hope that we've already begun to think simply as humans: anti-conformist, ironic humans full of a desire to live—this is the new human identity we propose.

What is identity for you?

I don't know; to be honest I've never looked for one . . . In my spiritual quest there is the awareness of abandoning the ego, and I think of an alien identity that doesn't correspond to the actual, current concept of identity.

What is fashion for you?

For me fashion is the act of transformation, being able to see yourself as others see you; it's not simply a matter of clothing. What

Alien Beauty Campaigns: Jake & Dinos Chapman Flag

Homme
Eau de Toilet
United Aliens
London-Milan

we're losing right now is precisely the centrality of this game of transformation . . . All this talk of luxury and style, only to then propose and present consumer products on a vast scale . . . It's sufficient to think of the metastasizing mania of multiplying the brand across the clothing, a culture of nouveaux riche who boast of the price, not the class . . . The worst of them all are Gucci, Calvin Klein, and Guess, but the list is endless . . . what I propose isn't fashion, it's the anemia of fashion. It's clear to everyone that what they want is to make money, not fashion. What we have begun to do is try to return to the magic of getting dressed, to recuperate the cult of beauty, in such a way that fashion becomes a form of relating between human beings; only in these terms can fashion be very important in society. Our work is a form of disruption, a movement against the large production companies, who want to homogenize people in order to transform them into wearers of consumer objects on a large scale, making them pay for the idea of luxury and privilege. I studied in Paris and learned that fashion is a sort of testimony that passes from hand to hand, a testimony of style, of refinement, of unique pieces: just think of the great French couturiers.

What is art for you?

It's the personal obsession of life, it's the creation of oneself, it's the creation of one's own destiny, and of one's own life . . . even here it's not a matter of just producing simple objects.

Which fashion designers seduce you?

Lagerfeld, Azzedine Alaïa, Vivienne Westwood, Coco Chanel, Fortuny, Capucci, Pucci, Missoni, Madame Gres, Christian Dior, Gaultier, Margiela, McQueen . . . the great ones, the ones who have succeeded at expressing the sense of fashion and not just a vulgar economic interest.

Which, on the other hand, are the ones you can't stand?

All the rest: those who in the name of fashion are just worried about increasing the number of examples and models in their messy mass of stuff.

Your philosophy is mainly based on a particular art/fashion relationship, and in your group there are artists, poets, and philosophers. But what, for you all, is the art/fashion relationship?

It's us, United Aliens! All jokes aside, I strongly believe that this is the future of fashion. Art has always existed, and not just as a type of commerce. Today fashion has to be part of a series of prestigious choices and not identify itself only with consumer products; in the same way art has to be on our bodies, in our way of living, in our repertory of images . . . and not simply in the houses of collectors or in museums.

Jasmine Guinness, hair-making Cosmo Jenks & Alien Holistic Couture

UA Fashion, Photo Roxanne Low

Alien

Veruschka in an Alien outfit

250

A.F.S.
ANTI-FEAR SPRAY

United Aliens London

Alien Beauty Campaigns. Photo Donna Trope

Kean Etro, 1998. Photo Roberto Orlandi

Etro

The first and foremost characteristic of Kean Etro is the lightness spoken of by Italo Calvino in his *Six Memos for the Next Millennium*. Historical intimations and alchemical fusions characterize his incessant investigation. A repertory of fairytale imagery, puns, texts, and sophisticated, ethereal images from one of the most original Italian fashion designers who has known how to "contaminate" a historic fashion house with contemporary tensions.

interview by FAM

FAM: How would you define yourself?
Kean Etro: I would define myself as a researcher . . . I studied medieval history and then found myself here, within a structure like Etro, very "establishment" and very "British," and I understood that perhaps I could do something by following my personal behavioral code, a code that reminded me of a "provenience," of deep roots. I began to appreciate the value of business archetypes, created perhaps unconsciously, but wherein you find things . . . funny, and ironic.
What does it mean to work today for 2002? Is it a premonition, a prophecy, a gamble?
To think of 2002 is first of all to marvel; to see a drawing, smell a scent, reread a book, discover a light . . . and, together with Jacopo, my brother, to allow myself to be taken by a form of enthusiasm that makes the love for an idea, for something that must take form, bloom. For me the concept of joy is very important, as is the concept of color. You know, color inspires

S/S 1998 - Photo Christopher Griffith

fear because it's not part of our daily lives. Munari, who together with Calder and Manzoni is one of my favorite artists, asked himself how on earth in 1956 we could still be bound to warmongering colors, to the colors of tanks and armored cars, to these grey, boring human machines . . . And it's still like that. Color is a great symbol, the symbol of true luxury, the symbol an enthusiastic child's joy.

Are there some words in your dictionary that you value more than others?
Self-irony, game, lightness . . . I have a lot of respect and admiration for the world of childhood, a world of colors, scents, touch—a world made up of an overwhelming sensorial input, which calls for a strong bodily presence—a world still very much alive within me. I continue to feel wonder and am fascinated by the discoveries that day by day I manage to make. The first book I read was *The Baron in the Trees*; at first it was very difficult, I was almost forced into it by my mother, but then it became a delightful read, one that I'm still passionate about. Just as with *The Little Prince*, one of the greatest visions regarding transitions, one of the best voyages of humankind . . . It's definitely a very visionary work, and yet remains closer to reality than one might believe . . . There is something marvelous about the game, about being able to let oneself be transported into parallel worlds, even if personally I'm fascinated by our everyday world as well, by

253

S/S 1999. Photo Michael Woolley

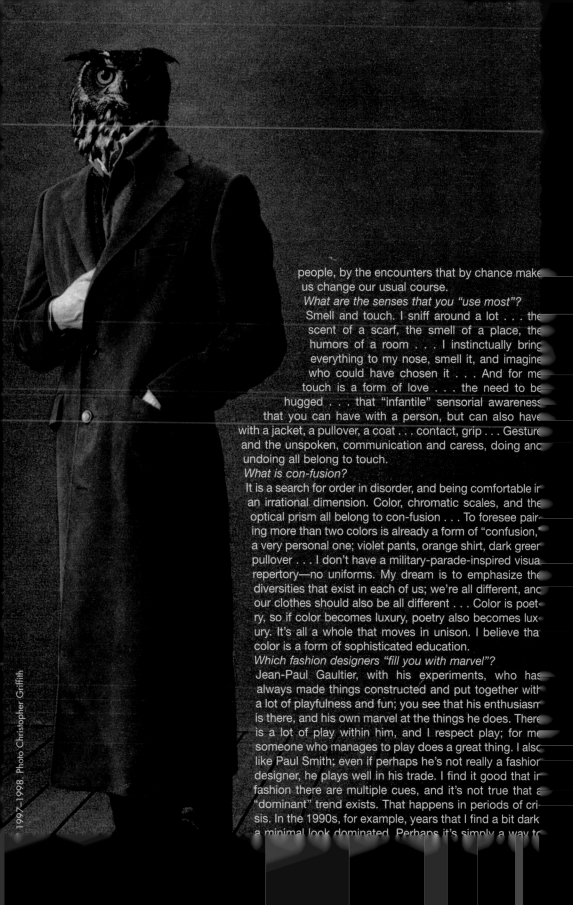

people, by the encounters that by chance make
us change our usual course.

What are the senses that you "use most"?

Smell and touch. I sniff around a lot . . . the
scent of a scarf, the smell of a place, the
humors of a room . . . I instinctually bring
everything to my nose, smell it, and imagine
who could have chosen it . . . And for me
touch is a form of love . . . the need to be
hugged . . . that "infantile" sensorial awareness
that you can have with a person, but can also have
with a jacket, a pullover, a coat . . . contact, grip . . . Gesture
and the unspoken, communication and caress, doing and
undoing all belong to touch.

What is con-fusion?

It is a search for order in disorder, and being comfortable in
an irrational dimension. Color, chromatic scales, and the
optical prism all belong to con-fusion . . . To foresee pairing more than two colors is already a form of "confusion,"
a very personal one; violet pants, orange shirt, dark green
pullover . . . I don't have a military-parade-inspired visual
repertory—no uniforms. My dream is to emphasize the
diversities that exist in each of us; we're all different, and
our clothes should also be all different . . . Color is poetry, so if color becomes luxury, poetry also becomes luxury. It's all a whole that moves in unison. I believe that
color is a form of sophisticated education.

Which fashion designers "fill you with marvel"?

Jean-Paul Gaultier, with his experiments, who has
always made things constructed and put together with
a lot of playfulness and fun; you see that his enthusiasm
is there, and his own marvel at the things he does. There
is a lot of play within him, and I respect play; for me
someone who manages to play does a great thing. I also
like Paul Smith; even if perhaps he's not really a fashion
designer, he plays well in his trade. I find it good that in
fashion there are multiple cues, and it's not true that a
"dominant" trend exists. That happens in periods of crisis. In the 1990s, for example, years that I find a bit dark,
a minimal look dominated. Perhaps it's simply a way to

1997–1998. Photo Christopher Griffith

What are the countries that fascinate you the most?
I love Japan; it's one of the few places where I wouldn't mind living for a while, because I've learned to breathe their air, which is both animistic and technological at the same time. Even if I shun the attitude toward work that is in force in companies there, which is truly dictatorial. I like the simplicity with which daily life there is organized; traffic lights, for example, have a microchip that reads the quantity of traffic—they're not preset to change every seven seconds!—and if there's a kilometer-long line it lets that kilometer flow through . . . There are little signs of respect and expediency,

and a way of emphasizing the flexibility of the material . . .
What do you allow to contaminate you the most?
For me the most powerful matrix of suggestion and sensorial involvement lies in books; you let yourself be transported, you let yourself traverse words. The contamination can be activated by any element whatsoever, as long as you let yourself go . . . Sometimes it begins with a thread . . . you touch it, and it's soft, swollen, impalpable, and you enter into a baby's crib . . . or into the heart of the 1950s . . . you move again and you're a puff . . . a sofa in a warm living room . . . There's a logic of crossing boundaries, a warmth that isn't absolute but is growing; a non-Aristotelian logic, not black or white, but that immaterial grey that you then find applied.

Images from the *Disegni Animati* exhibition of Philip Kwame Apagya for Etro, Milan, 2000

Frankie Morello

In 1998 Maurizio Modica and Piero Gigliotti founded the FRANKIE MORELLO brand, characterized by a style that develops their continually evolving quest. Since 2001 the women's line has accompanied the men's line, which had already established them on the market, and was met with immediate success.

Maurizio Modica and Piero Gigliotti. Photo Antonio Maniscalco

by
FAUSTO CALETTI

Arriving at fashion through a desire for personal change, Maurizio Modica and Piero Gigliotti founded the Frankie Morello brand in 1998. This project was born of their creative meeting, which early on translated itself into a desire to invent a studio-house-atelier where they could design and sell fine men's clothing. Their first fashion show was for the Spring–Summer 1999 season; they decided to conceal themselves behind a pseudonym that would make people think of an Italian emigrant with something irreverent and goofy about him—something irremediably unfashionable and un-chic.

They set out to create men's lines because they thought that there was still something that remained yet to be invented, and immediately translated their ideas into a clear and noteworthy stylistic matrix. They formulated a very sought-after—but not purely cutting-edge conceptual—basic line, and juxtaposed the most simple, often cotton-based, fabrics with alternative materials like the colored latex they used for the bathing suits in their first show. Being very attentive to present their collections in a well-thought-out manner, for the Spring–Summer 2000 season they set the fashion show amid a stage of artificial snow, and in this way proposed a winter in mid-summer. Their love for representation and theatrical performance undoubtedly came from Maurizio's contribution, which included, in addition to a collaboration with the Alessi Studio Center, a past life in theatrical dance. From season to season their contacts grew, and from the thousand garments made and sold on their own at the first presentation they arrived at the honor of being fea-

tured in the most beautiful boutiques throughout the world. As spontaneous and simple as their fashion, they always thought of a young man who constructs his wardrobe over the passage of seasons without ever abandoning comfort and irony.

The Summer 2001 season was marked by a 1950s, rock 'n' roll, Vichy plaid style. It was the birth of the women's collection, which reached an immediate success and was published in the most stylish magazines. The game continued with the collections of the following Winter season. For men there was *Frankie Morello's Restaurant*, where, on a catwalk set up like a long and well-furnished table, strutted a carefree, liberated collection that offered up fast recipes made with a single ingredient, like corduroy from head-to-toe, including accessories, or multiple flavors for a "moody" outfit.

That season's woman was a girl who has fun arranging clothes in her mother's closet and messing up formal order by playing with different pieces and

Summer 2002. Photo Lorenzo Marcucci

colors. Everything proposed in each collection aimed not to upset or over-turn, but rather to evolve toward new explorations that are absolutely possi-ble—eccentricities included—in daily life.

Frankie Morello is a brand with a short history behind it, but it has already succeeded in giving form to a clear idea that is making up its widespread success—the offering of a basic yet non-traditional fashion that avoids the elitist sophistications that so often characterize young brands.

F/W 2001–2002. Photo Lorenzo Marcucci

Comme des Garçons

Rei Kawakubo, the Japanese founder of the Comme des Garçons brand, is known throughout the fashion world for her obsession with fabrics. In this previously unpublished piece by Fausto Caletti, her extraordinary capacity to hybridize Western asymmetries with traditional Asian forms is underlined.

by FAUSTO CALETTI

S/S 1995

263

The iconoclastic and ironic Rei Kawakubo invented the Comme des Garçons brand at the end of the 1960s. The foundation of the business dates back to 1973, but it was only in the early 1980s that it began to hold fashion shows in Paris—shows that shocked the public. She was immediately associated with the thread of "Japanese in Paris," so typical of the period, who opposed the Western concept of physicality. Rei opened her first boutique in 1983 in the French capital, creating a new poetics.

Her early style was made up of highly studied cuts that were clumsy in appearance; her paper models were so articulated that they resembled works of art, so much so that in 1997 they were presented at the Florence Biennale. Absolutely obsessed with fabric, her creations often began with the raw material. Preciousness acquired a different value with "Comme"; the refinement and worth of her elaborations tended to create looks that were worn and torn, holed, faded, and discolored— the exact opposite of the decorative style that was at an apogee in the early 1980s. Her techniques went into the history books; master of plush and treatments that modify the value of any and every material, Rei Kawakubo finds the perfect balance only with black.

Up until 1989 her fashion is almost entirely black, or at the most a gray/blue with a few touches of ecru and neutral tones, since nothing must attract one's glance and take attention away from the form. The obsession for modifying human anatomy became a constant in her

F/W 1995–1996

extremely personal stylistic format. For the Spring–Summer 1997 season she invented the famous *Vichy* dresses, with deforming bulges in every imaginable place, in a search for independent forms. Rei Kawakubo negated every past experience, and desired to create only the new; throughout the 1980s there were no revivals, no citations, no recalling of any other period.

1989 was the year of change. Her style appeared new and victorious in a completely colored fashion show. While remaining true to herself, Rei wanders in the most audacious chromatics. From this date forward her references to past periods, retro, and typical motifs are much more numerous. Nevertheless, in her design nothing tends toward the reconstruction of a principle, and the typical irony of the brand once again comes forward, desecrating polka dots, Sangallo lace, couture pinstripes, drapery, the naïve style, and the baroque. The Comme des Garçons woman is ageless, an eternal little girl who has fun daring, and pays no heed to the female phantasms offered by every other designer. Her style is a little infantile, and yet cultured and sophisticated. Rei Kawakubo's range of motion doesn't limit itself to fashion, but covers every form that regards design. In the late 1980s she designed a furniture series in wood and aluminum for Pallucco, foreshadowing the ascetic and minimalist taste that would characterize the following decade.

Always attentive to every detail, Kawakubo was one of the first to choose an advertising campaign that focused on suggestion without

F/W 1992–1993

267

showing the actual product; she was a forerunner in opening stores that were true concept stores, closer to art galleries than to boutiques. The desire to set herself apart, which is absolutely natural for Rei, brought her to the point of changing even the way in which she presented her collections. The catwalk was replaced by bona fide performances and, for the men's fashion shows, she chose amateur models that were sometimes neither young nor beautiful. Among those who have taken part in her shows are Francesco Clemente, who was also a protagonist of an advertising campaign, Dennis Hopper, and Robert Rauschenberg. She also achieved preeminence for talent scouting young designers. A philosophical, audacious form of subversion is the main motto of "Comme," which has proven itself capable of expressing even contradictory concepts while still remaining true to itself.

Costumes for a dance performance in collaboration with the Cunningham Dance Foundation, 1997. Photo Timothy Greenfield-Sanders, courtesy of Comme des Garçons, Paris, and the Cunningham Dance Foundation, New York

aleXsandro Palombo

F/W 2001–2002 Photo Lorenzo Alisio

Imagine, as if you were under a spell, being transported back in time; for the first time you feel the earth under your feet, you smell the strong scents that only the earth can create, you admire the colors, and let yourself go in this seductive wave of ancient flavors and rites.

interview by TITTI BOTTICCHIO

All this and even more is just a little summary of what you can perceive in the collection of aleXsandro Palombo. It is precisely his roots in the Salento that formed and marked the fashion designer's childhood. The rich agricultural and earthy upbringing from his grandfather, the continual presence of his grandmother's embroidery pillow, the days spent watching his aunts and relatives finish making their trousseau, the songs . . . aleXsandro is then able, over time, to make all of this come back to life, bringing the *pizzicata* to the catwalk, the magnificent craft productions, openwork laces, ancient embroideries, the laces of Padre Pio . . . He brings back to mind the sacrifices and sweat of a past generation as if time had stopped, and by becoming a timeless fashion designer himself. He brings us back to those hot days when people harvested tobacco, sweaty yet happy, where at times among the common people one found looks of folly, the look of those who had just been bitten by the cursed tarantula, to then guide us with his subtle intuition through the *tarantolati* of 2000 and—why not?—even farther into the future.

Titti Botticchio: What does being a fashion designer mean to you?
aleXsandro Palombo: To live on the edge of emotions, perceive their soul, and transmit it into costume without ever losing sight of the sense of reality. To possess a great humility, and know what it means to go all the way.
What are you most influenced by?
Art has always had an important reflection in my fashion; I have structured entire collections through studies comparing and contrasting Lecce's very rich baroque with the minimalist misery of the Salento's *masseria* farm complexes. I wanted to understand how on earth two architectural elements that were so completely opposite could live together in total harmony, expressing a profound and pleasant visual and chromatic equilibrium. I used the results of my studies in the elaboration of the lines and colors of my collections. I strongly believe in instinct, and I try to perceive every glance, every gesture, every single detail that makes up the daily life of the individual in order to give my garments a natural direction.
I know that you love provocation: do you see yourself as a provocateur or someone who is provoked?

My eyes are the testimonials of time, my heart of the emotion of the moment . . . Someone wrote about me and defined me a contested, admired, and sometimes reproachful fashion designer. One thing is for certain: that my desire to fight is stronger than fear, that I hate conformity, and all this naturally makes my fashion one born of revolt and challenge—the revolt against a de facto system that limits young creative people with settings steeped in corporatism, obscuring the freedom of expression. The challenge lies in the unavoidability of this thing. If by provocation you mean telling the reality of things, well then I'm a provocateur. I am convinced that if a group of professionally selected and firmly convinced people practice this trade with heart, soul, and passion, serving only the buyer, they can obtain from him enough to keep their business going without needing to put themselves in the shadow of a protector. Well-to-do conformists have defined me a dreamer, and naysayers have defined me a madman. I just feel like a sensible person.
In the last show your models walked to the rhythm of the tarantella; do you care to explain that?
It's the centuries old phenomenon of the Salento's *tarantismo*: the tarantula bites and poisons the soul, in addition to the body, but then the music, through dance and colors, frees the victim from an otherwise unavoidable death. The only remedy to help cure the people *pizzicate*, or bitten, was actually to wait until the dose of poison wore out, venting themselves through dance. The healers were also called "pharmacists," common people who on the necessary occasions played four instruments until reaching the point of exhaustion: a guitar, a tambourine, an accordion, and a violin. Optical white, which the bitten woman was dressed in, and the white linens that delimited the ceremonial perimeter of the dance, symbolized the purity that, beyond just the body, relaxed even the soul. The dance could last for days, up until when the spider's injected venom lost its efficacy, burnt by the sweat and sacrifice of the *tarantolata* (bite victim) and the musicians. My women carry with them the sensuality of that music—a tornado of femininity, and a great and powerful evoker of memories.

What is your relationship with the Salento's artisanal crafts?
A labor-intensive project: to give back life to the very ancient techniques of craftsmanship that are typical of my region, but by now threatened by extinction. Openwork lace and cross-stitch are just some of their magical techniques that charge each garment with a great timeless value, a luxury to rediscover and reinterpret.

Artisan's engravings, tailor's embroideries, all emphasized by a passionate style, a muse: how would you describe your muse?
I believe it's no longer the age of the muses, we all represent time and we all interpret it; my fashion simply takes the human side of every woman who carries drama and happiness within, in a continual chain of memories, as a testimonial of our time and interpreter of the great past—gypsies of time, *tarantolate* who at every moment are ready to be themselves, anywhere and anyhow . . .

What is one of the most incredible places you'd like to have your woman put on a fashion show?
In the heart of the people.

Padre Pio, Mother Theresa, Saint Paul . . . a fashion to be looked for, to be rediscovered: the sacred or the profane? aleXsandro Palombo as Pax Christi . . .
Certainly these are the three cardinal figures of my work: the Apulia of Padre Pio, the man-medium of the twentieth century; the generosity of Mother Theresa, woman of the neighboring and poor land of Albania; and Saint Paul, protector of the *tarantolati* of the Salento region. My fashion touches on the sacred in a "territorial" way, to underline the uses and customs of the people of Salento. My signature is aleXsandro Palombo, with the X uppercase like the P, to signify the famous Latin symbol for *Pax Christi*, a symbol present in all the sacred baroque constructions of the Salento. This is a fashion that seeks out the ethnicity of the land, underlining its anthropological part, in a precise philosophical path that leads to the rediscovery of ancient and magical values.

Do you think of yourself as a fashion designer, an artist, a philosopher, or a religious figure?
Those are demanding words for a farmer of fashion! I think of myself as a man who is free to think, look, and create. My depth isn't, and never will be, in the label, but lies instead in the safe-deposit box of memories, emotions, and all those things that are dear to me and that I'll always carry within.

How do you relate to so-called compromises, and in what way are you contaminated by them? And what, for you, are the true values, if there are any?
When you grow up in a bitter South where looks are profound, where wrinkles tell of the hard work of suffering, and where respect becomes penitence, well then compromise becomes difficult, if not with life itself. Many times in my work I have seen Mr. Compromise pass by; he had an ascetic look and smooth skin, manicured hands and a tuned voice . . . that Mr. Compromise doesn't have, and never has had, the time to stay at my side for any longer than a little chit-chat. Life is to be conquered, it's like a great mountain, it is to be climbed with respect and profound sacrifice.

Projects for the future?
To continue doing what I feel without impositions of any sort. My fashion has no masters, not even me.

Antonio Marras

Among the characteristics of Antonio Marras one finds Byzantine preciousness and volumes derived from traditional Sardinian costumes. Aged fabrics of muslin are made richer with ruches, georgettes, and macramé lace reinvented in fashions that overturn the forms' traditional use.

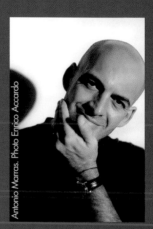

Antonio Marras. Photo Enrico Accardo

interview by FRANCESCA CARAFFINI

Francesca Caraffini: It seems that there is a major rediscovery of Mediterranean traditions in fashion at the moment . . . How are you taking part in this phenomenon?
Antonio Marras: Being Sardinian, I believe that this is a natural characteristic of mine. The Italian and Mediterranean matrix springs forth and becomes visible in everything I do.
A culture derived from migration and stratification . . . a mix that has perhaps foreshadowed what will be one of the sole possibilities for the future?
A true union between different races and peoples is what I would like to see become a concrete reality, and is probably what we all hope for. Union—certainly not the tragedies that are now taking place. That's something I really don't like to talk about in these "discourses" on fashion, because they're a matter of extremely grave and serious phenomena, and the field of fashion, however important it is, appears very futile in such a context. They're undoubtedly events and happenings that upset our lives and are transmitted into whatever one is doing, influencing it. What one can see today is the result of a mood connected to what is going on in the world.
There is an ever-stronger contamination between male and female in your latest collections . . .
Yes, this has always been a constant in my work; masculine fabrics adapted to feminine forms, or, on the contrary, extremely feminine fabrics rubbed up, dyed in tea, and destined to a use that differs greatly from the traditional one. I think that identity needs to be more open, more "practical," interchangeable. What I offer aspires to be an opportunity to live one's own identity more freely.
What inspires you most—earth, air, colors . . .?
The work that I do, which develops in a continual search for fabrics, materi-

F/W 2000–2001

als, objects, dresses, cinematic images, paintings, the theater . . . I dedicate myself only to the things that I like! It is perhaps a sort of limit, but it coincides precisely with my method of designing: overlapping layers, and strata of things that reconstruct themselves together.

Are there any artists you'd like to work with?

I have some loves, but unfortunately they've passed away: Giacometti and Burri. I am classic in my choices, but they're the ones I like the most—great

S/S 2002

revolutionaries and innovators, great poets and dreamers. They continue to exercise a special charm over me . . . then there's Kounellis, who always makes me feel very strong emotions, and Kiefer, who upsets me. They've marked my visual repertory, together, certainly, with Pina Bausch; I like everything about her way of understanding and thinking about dance.

Is the idea of working with cinema among the things you'd like to do in the future?

Yes, absolutely! I'd like to collaborate on a cinematographic project; this could beco... a new research direction for me.

S/S 2002

S/S 2002

Cinzia Ruggeri

Liquid-crystal fabrics, kinetic dresses, ball-shaped purses made of chicken leather, and grass, egg, and feather dresses . . . Here we approach Cinzia Ruggeri—the queen and inventor of extravagant and genial creations for dresses, design objects, and new horizons—at the safe distance of several years after her original and prescient presentations.

b y MARCO TAGLIAFIERRO

Cinzia Ruggeri. Photo Occhio Magico, Milan

Photo Occhio Magico, Milan

"Certain days, and it's not a given that they're the worst ones, Cinzia sets herself to raining," Dino Buzzati wrote in a story dedicated to Ms. Ruggeri, revealing her most intimate and hidden personality. The emphasis, together with the shock that accompanies it, is for her the passe-partout for a new, infinite dimension. The Cinzia Ruggeri of emphatic parties and the

283

Photo Occhio Magico, Milan

284

choreographies composed of eggs left to age under Chinese soil is the same as the Cinzia Ruggeri of the teardrop-carrier and warrior furniture, who for a while decided to investigate clothing as a means for expression. When she was asked, "If you were an outfit, what outfit would you be?" she replied, "I'd be simple, useful overalls, but ones that hide a small treasure sewn into the lining." Cinzia works with the emotions of the heart and the mind; on her shirts there are moveable appliqués with which one can play as people often do with their hair—for example, a heart to be pierced with an arrow tied to the end of a little cord. The intimate relationship with the materials she uses is expressed also through her love for slate, which she defines "the stone of memory"; a mineral that absorbs footprints and impressions, to then leave them behind when one least expects it. The non-place here is like the sole possible condition in which to think and work, but also to live—the wellbeing one feels in a clear, starlit night—are all parts of her. Bare moonscapes burnt by the sun and wind are one of her dimensions; Cinzia morbidly loves them, just as she loves African bread

Photo Occhio Magico, Milan

285

Photo Occhio Magico, Milan

and tripe, between those open pores she sees flowers and multicolored outgrowths sprout up, a regurgitation to swallow straightaway, an intimacy to show and then take back in a fit of modesty. She lives in a house with a sky-blue flooring, together with a virile molding of black velvet; the spider web curtains project toward the outside a mysterious light, and inside it is all a broil of feelings like the pot of a magic potion. Cinzia moves like a performer of affectivity, and dances out her feelings in a hybrid choreography between jazz and a baroque design sensibility.

bind me

packages, laces, and garters between fashion and art

Corsets and bandages, tapes and laces, tight and pulled; from art to fashion, there and back again, here are some elements that constrict us with seduction.

by FAUSTO CALETTI

Photo Yoshi Nishikawa

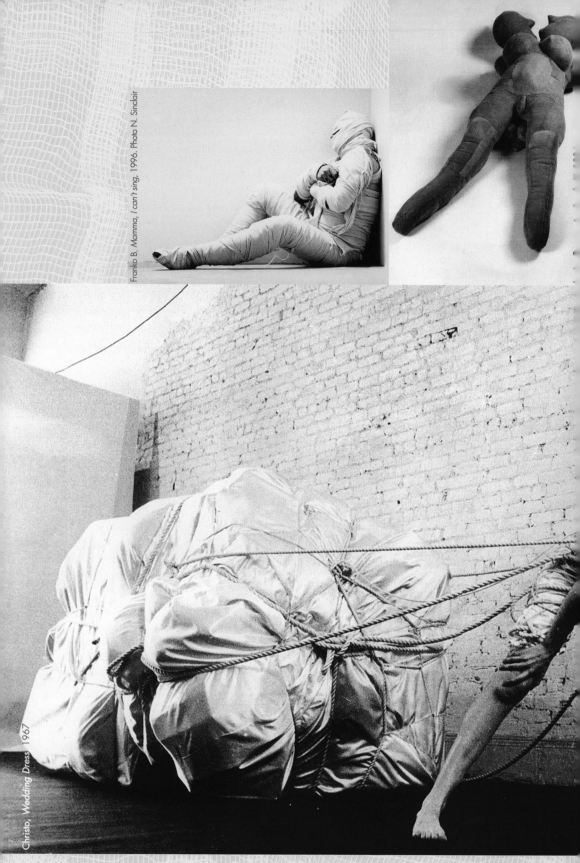

Franko B, *Mamma, I can't sing*, 1996. Photo N. Sinclair

Christo, *Wedding Dress* 1967

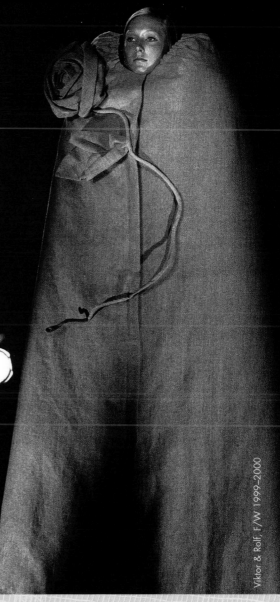

Man Ray, The enigma of Isidore Ducasse, 1920

Viktor & Rolf, F/W 1999–2000

Primitive man wore nothing more than his own skin and a loincloth, the **ancient Egyptians** bound their mummies with cotton gauzes, and the **ancient Greeks** and **Romans** held their peplum in place with long laces. Going backwards in time it is possible to note how atavistic the act of binding and using laces is. The desire and necessity to hold in place and straighten out clothing can be found even in the most **ancient farming tradi-**

tions. Laces and ribbons were used to adapt garments to various body types, modifying them in the simplest of ways.

And the **apron**? It is the emblematic example of a standard garment created simply with a piece of rectangular fabric and some ribbons, that can always be adapted and modified. Another type of lacing is that of **bikinis**, one of the most revolutionary inventions of the twentieth century. The 1970s version of the bikini, which has recently come back into fashion, is one big exhibi-

A double thread leading from art to fashion passing by bodies marked by the chains of seduction.

The creativity of artists and fashion designers, from the past and into the future, runs along the attraction of a tightly tied bond.

tion of laces that hold together the mythic "handkerchiefs."

The interpretation of this vestment is doubly sexy; the laces make the bikini seem even smaller, and give one the impression that the whole thing could come unlaced from one moment to the next. The sensuality of laces and ribbons is undeniable. In the early 1990s **Azzedine Alaïa**, the magician of the silhouette, created anatomical mini-dresses made of pure and simple ribbons. Nor did **Manolo Blahnik** miss out the chance to propose

Man Ray, Venus Restored, 1936

Mario Valentino advertising campaign. Photo: Lei Roretti

Jana Sterbak, Vest, 1992

sandals and shoes with laces to wrap around the ankles, with a wink to sadomasochism.

And one cannot leave out, when mentioning ties, idolatry and slavery; but it's enough to think of **Madonna** to avoid the risk of taking everything for granted. In a scene of her *Human Nature* music video she is surrounded by dancers in a "performance that binds," which transforms her into a painting straight out of a 1950s Hollywood

Gauzes, bandages, cords . . . hermetically enveloped bodies that take on resemblances of a chrysalis.

John Galliano, F/W 1986-1987. Photo Niall McInerney

Kiki Smith, *Siren*, 1994

musical. Laces, ribbons, and cords express meanings very close to human beings, in a seesawing between practical simplicity and subtle perversion. To tie oneself up, and bind oneself like a package or wrapping, is perhaps an unusual way of offering oneself up as a gift to the stupefied eyes of the world.

SOURCES

All of the articles published in this volume were taken from the magazines *Virus* and *Virus Mutations*:

WEAR YOUR HYBRIDIZATION: *Virus Mutations*, no. 9, December 1999
HELMUT NEWTON: *Virus*, no. 0, June 1993
ROMEO GIGLI: *Virus*, no. 3, November 1994
TED POLHEMUS: *Virus*, no. 4, April 1995
STEPHAN JANSON: *Virus*, no. 5, June 1995
LIZA BRUCE: *Virus*, no. 6, October 1995
ANN DEMEULEMEESTER: *Virus*, no. 7, March 1996
ALEXANDER MCQUEEN: *Virus*, no. 8, June 1997
ANNA MOLINARI: *Virus*, no. 10, January 1997
MARTIN MARGIELA: *Virus*, no. 8, June 1996
DAVID LA CHAPELLE: *Virus Mutations*, no. 0, May 1997
VICTOR BELLAISH: *Virus Mutations*, no. 2, February 1998
BARE-BREASTED: *Virus Mutations*, no. 10, February 2000
JEAN-PAUL GAULTIER: *Virus Mutations*, no. 0, May 1997
JESSICA OGDEN: *Virus Mutations*, no. 1, October 1998
VIVIENNE WESTWOOD: *Virus Mutations*, no. 1, October 1997
MATT LEHITKA: *Virus Mutations*, no. 2, February 1998
NAOKI TAKIZAWA: *Virus Mutations*, no. 5, December 1998
COSTUME NATIONAL: *Virus Mutations*, no. 3, May 1998
HELEN STOREY: *Virus Mutations*, no. 3, May 1998
MANUEL VASON: *Virus Mutations*, no. 9, December 1999
DIESEL: *Virus Mutations*, no. 3, May 1998
RANKIN: *Virus Mutations*, no. 4, September 1998
WALTER VAN BEIRENDONCK: *Virus Mutations*, no. 5, December 1998
ALAN HRANITELJ: *Virus Mutations*, no. 6, March 1999
ARMATURE: *Virus Mutations*, no. 15, January 2001
PEPI'S: *Virus Mutations*, no. 6, March 1999
FAUSTO PUGLISI: *Virus Mutations*, no. 6, March 1999
TRISTAN WEBBER: *Virus Mutations*, no. 6, March 1999
KEI KAGAMI: *Virus Mutations*, no. 7, June 1999
MANUEL ALBARRAN: *Virus Mutations*, no. 7, June 1999
CAROL CHRISTIAN POELL: *Virus Mutations*, no. 8, September 1999
JOHN WILLIE: *Virus Mutations*, no. 8, September 1999
ALAIN MIKLI: *Virus Mutations*, no. 8, September 1999
ANTONIO BERARDI: *Virus Mutations*, no. 9, December 1999
STEP BY STEP: *Virus Mutations*, no. 15, January 2001
CYBERDOG: *Virus Mutations*, no. 10, February 2000
THIERRY MUGLER: *Virus Mutations*, no. 10, February 2000
AZZEDINE ALAÏA: *Virus Mutations*, no. 11, April 2000
DIRK BIKKEMBERGS: *Virus Mutations*, no. 12, June 2000
MONICA COPPOLA: *Virus Mutations*, no. 13, September 2000
JEREMY SCOTT: *Virus Mutations*, no. 14, November 2000
UNITED ALIENS: *Virus Mutations*, no. 14, November 2000
ETRO: *Virus Mutations*, no. 15, January 2001
FRANKIE MORELLO: *Virus Mutations*, no. 18, July 2001
COMME DES GARÇONS: *Virus Mutations*, no. 19, September 2001
ALEXSANDRO PALOMBO: *Virus Mutations*, no. 19, September 2001
ANTONIO MARRAS: *Virus Mutations*, no. 20, November 2001
CINZIA RUGGERI: *Virus Mutations*, no. 20, November 2001
BIND ME: *Virus Mutations*, no. 11, April 2000